COOKIES
for kids

COOKIES
for kids

50 fabulous, fun recipes
to cook with your family

JOANNA FARROW

southwater

This edition is published by Southwater, an imprint of
Anness Publishing Limited, 108 Great Russell Street,
London WC1B 3NA
info@anness.com; www.annesspublishing.com
twitter: @Anness_Books

If you like the images in this book and would like to investigate using
them for publishing, promotions or advertising, please visit our website
www.practicalpictures.com for more information.

© Anness Publishing Ltd 2015

Publisher: Joanna Lorenz
Senior Editor: Susannah Blake
Photographer: Frank Adam
Home Economist: Jenny White
Designer: Paul Oakley
Stylist: Helen Trent
Production Controller: Rosanna Anness

A CIP catalogue record for this book is available from the British Library

COOK'S NOTES
Bracketed terms are intended for American readers.
For all recipes, quantities are given in both metric and imperial measures and, where appropriate, in standard cups and spoons. Follow
one set of measures, but not a mixture, because they are not interchangeable.
Standard spoon and cup measures are level. 1 tsp = 5ml, 1 tbsp = 15ml, 1 cup = 250ml/8fl oz.
Australian standard tablespoons are 20ml. Australian readers should use 3 tsp in place of 1 tbsp for measuring small quantities.
American pints are 16fl oz/2 cups. American readers should use 20fl oz/2.5 cups in place of 1 pint when measuring liquids.
Electric oven temperatures in this book are for conventional ovens. When using a fan oven, the temperature will probably need to be
reduced by about 10–20°C/20–40°F. Since ovens vary, you should check with your manufacturer's instruction book for guidance.
Medium (US large) eggs are used unless otherwise stated.

PUBLISHER'S NOTE
All the recipes in this book have been created with simplicity, effectiveness and fun in mind. However, there are some stages in the
recipes where potentially dangerous utensils or equipment are needed. The level of adult supervision of children using this book will
depend on the age and ability of the child, but we advise that adult supervision is always preferable and vital if the recipe calls for the
use of sharp knives and electrical equipment. Although the advice and information in this book are believed to be accurate and true
at the time of going to press, neither the authors nor the publisher can accept any legal responsibility or liability for any errors or
omissions that may be made nor for any inaccuracies nor for any harm or injury that comes about from following instructions or advice
in this book.

Contents

Introduction

Making Cookies

There's nothing better than coming home from school to a freshly baked cookie and a glass of milk. Whether it is the taste and texture, or the shape and size, there's no doubt that kids of all ages love cookies.

Although the cookies you make at home are likely to be high in sugar and fat, they are often a healthier option than store-bought ones. A simple cookie made from unsalted (sweet) butter, sugar, eggs and flour will always be better for your kids than a mass-produced cookie full of chemicals added to enhance its flavour, colour and texture.

If you are catering for a child with special dietary needs, such as a gluten- or dairy-intolerance, it is often easier to bake your own cookies. This way, you know that they can safely enjoy the treat, too.

Below: Decorating cookies with kids' names can be a fun idea for children's parties or for a special tea.

GETTING KIDS INVOLVED

One of the really great things about cookies is that kids love making them as much as they do eating them. Most cookies are very simple to make and can be the perfect way to introduce your child to cooking. Even quite small children can get involved – perhaps pressing cookie cutters into a sheet of rolled-out dough, drizzling icing over a baked cookie, or sticking on sweets (candies) to decorate them.

Making and baking cookies can also create a fun environment in which your child can learn. Reading and following a recipe, measuring out ingredients accurately, rolling and shaping dough and decorating the finished cookies are all valuable lessons for a child. Making cookies can also be a good way to learn about basic hygiene and kitchen safety such as washing hands, tying back long hair and taking care when handling hot pans and trays.

Above: Kids love getting involved in decorating cookies, adding their own individual touches to each one.

As children become more experienced in the kitchen, they will be able to make quite complex cookies, and cope with more fiddly techniques and decorations.

TAKING CARE WITH NUTS
Nutty cookies are enormously popular, but always remember that eating a cookie containing nuts can be life-threatening for someone with a nut allergy. If you make cookies that contain nuts, always check that none of the recipients has a nut allergy before offering them a cookie. If in doubt, don't take the risk and make a batch of nut-free cookies instead. As well as the risk of allergy, be aware that small children can choke on whole nuts.

DIFFERENT DOUGHS

There are several ways to make cookie dough. Each one produces a different type of dough that can be shaped and baked in different ways and gives different results.

All-in-one method

This method produces a soft dough that is usually spooned on to a baking sheet and then baked. All the ingredients are placed in a bowl or food processor and mixed until thoroughly combined. Always use butter or margarine at room temperature for this method.

Creaming method

This is similar to the all-in-one method but the ingredients are combined in stages. It produces a similar soft, spoonable dough; the dough can sometimes be chilled, then rolled out. Soft butter and sugar are beaten together, then the eggs and dry ingredients are mixed in to form a dough.

Below: Some doughs can be shaped into balls, which will spread out during cooking to make pretty, round cookies.

Rubbing-in method

This popular technique makes a firm dough that may be rolled out and cut into shapes, or pressed into a tin (pan), then cut into bars or squares once baked. Chilled butter or margarine is rubbed into dry ingredients, either using the fingertips, or in a food processor. Eggs or milk are then often added to bind the mixture together.

Melting method

This method makes a very soft, spoonable dough that will spread out when dropped on to a baking sheet, making flat cookies such as florentines. Butter, syrup and sugar are heated together until melted, then dry ingredients are mixed in. The melting method can also be used to make no-bake cookies.

Whisked method

This method makes a soft mixture that can be dropped on to a baking sheet. It produces thin, crisp

Below: Bar cookies can be made in a large flat tin, then cut into squares once they have been baked.

> **WHAT'S IN A NAME?**
> Around the world, cookies are known by different names. In many parts of the world, cookies are known as biscuits. However, in the United States a "biscuit" is actually more like a scone. In Scotland, the term "cookie" is used to describe a sweet bread bun, filled with cream or covered in thick icing.

cookies such as fortune cookies. Egg whites are whisked until they hold soft peaks, then sugar and other dry ingredients are folded in.

FINISHING TOUCHES

Decorating cookies will add to the fun of cookie-making. Decorations can be as simple or as complex as you like, from sticking on a few sweets (candies) with a little icing, or piping intricate patterns or faces.

Below: A mixture of breakfast cereal and melted chocolate can be chilled to make delicious no-bake cookies.

Cookie Ingredients

Most cookies are made from a few basic ingredients: a fat, such as butter, sugar, flour and sometimes eggs. Additional ingredients such as flavourings or dried fruit and nuts may also be stirred into the dough.

FATS

The most popular fat used in cookie-making is butter, but other types of hard fat can also be used.

BUTTER This gives cookies a rich flavour and a warm golden colour. Unsalted (sweet) butter is usually favoured for cookie-making. It is important that the butter is at the right temperature for the recipe. For rubbed-in cookies, butter should be cold and firm; it should be removed from the refrigerator about 5 minutes before use. For the creaming method, butter should be at room temperature.

MARGARINE This fat won't give as rich a flavour as butter, but it gives adequate results. For most cookies, you should use the solid block type made specifically for baking. Soft-tub margarine is far too soft for making rubbed-in cookies, but it can be used for both the creaming method and the all-in-one method.

SUGAR

An essential ingredient in virtually every type of cookie, sugar adds sweetness, flavour and texture. Different sugars produce different results, so always choose the right type for the recipe. It is best to use unrefined sugars whenever possible.

GRANULATED SUGAR This sugar has large, coarse granules. It can be used in rubbed-in mixtures or as a crunchy cookie topping.

CASTER/SUPERFINE SUGAR Use this fine granular sugar for creaming with butter to make light-textured cookies. It is also ideal for meringue mixtures and melted mixtures. It is sometimes sprinkled over cookies.

ICING/CONFECTIONERS' SUGAR A fine, powdery sugar that is mainly used to make icings and fillings and for dusting over baked cookies. It is also incorporated in doughs used for piped cookies.

SOFT BROWN SUGAR This is refined white sugar that has been tossed in molasses or syrup to colour and flavour it; the darker the colour, the more intense the flavour will be. Soft brown sugar produces a moister cookie than white sugar; the two are not interchangeable in recipes.

Left: It is easier to use diced butter in recipes, whether melting, blending with or rubbing it into other ingredients.

GOLDEN SUGARS Pale golden caster and granulated sugars are available in most supermarkets and can be used in the same way as white. Golden sugars may be refined or unrefined.

Demerara/raw sugar This unrefined golden sugar has large granules and a slight toffee flavour. It is seldom used in cookie doughs, except those made by the melting method or if a very crunchy texture is required, but it is excellent for sprinkling over cookies before baking to produce a crunchy topping.

Muscovado/molasses sugar This fine, soft-textured sugar can be light or dark brown and produces cookies with a slight caramel flavour.

Molasses sugar Similar in taste and texture to muscovado sugar, this is slightly moister and has a stronger treacly flavour.

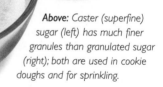

Above: Caster (superfine) sugar (left) has much finer granules than granulated sugar (right); both are used in cookie doughs and for sprinkling.

Left: Plain (all-purpose) flour is the most popular flour used in cookie making.

FLOUR

There are a variety of different flours used for cookies.

PLAIN/ALL-PURPOSE FLOUR The low gluten content of this flour produces crumbly textured cookies.

SELF-RAISING/SELF-RISING FLOUR This flour contains leavening agents that make cookies spread and rise during baking, giving them a lighter, airier texture.

WHOLEMEAL/WHOLE-WHEAT FLOUR The coarser texture of this flour gives quite dense results. It also absorbs more liquid than white flour, so recipes should be adjusted if it is substituted for white flour.

BROWN/WHEATMEAL FLOUR Containing 80 per cent of the bran and wheat germ, this is finer than wholemeal and has a milder taste.

GLUTEN-FREE BAKING
Specially produced gluten-free and wheat-free flour can be used to make cookies, as can any of the naturally gluten-free flours such as buckwheat, cornmeal, potato flour, rice flour and soya flour.

RAISING AGENTS

To produce a cookie with a lighter texture, raising agents such as bicarbonate of soda (baking soda) or baking powder are often added to the dough along with the flour. As the cookie bakes, the raising agents react with the moisture in the cookie mixture, producing tiny air bubbles that help the cookie to spread and rise.

EGGS

Adding eggs to cookie mixtures can either help to bind together dry ingredients, or prevent rolled cookie dough from spreading and losing its shape during baking.

When adding eggs to cookie mixtures, the eggs should be at room temperature. Add egg yolks or beaten eggs to creamed mixtures a little at a time, beating well. If the mixture starts to curdle, beat in 15ml/1 tbsp sifted flour.

LIQUID SWEETENERS

Below: Eggs can be used to bind together ingredients or set doughs.

Some recipes use sweet syrups as well as sugar, which add flavour and texture. They are most widely used in melted cookie mixtures.

GOLDEN/LIGHT CORN SYRUP This can add a moist, sticky texture to cookies and is often used in no-bake cookies to bind ingredients.

TREACLE/MOLASSES This dark syrup has a stronger flavour than golden syrup and is slightly bitter.

OTHER LIQUID SWEETENERS These include honey, maple syrup, malt extract and glucose syrup.

FLAVOURINGS

Above: All kinds of chocolate are used as a flavouring for cookies.

As well as the rich taste produced from the basic cookie ingredients, additional flavourings can also be added. Chocolate is one of the most popular but vanilla, lemon, orange, and warm spices such as cinnamon are often used.

Additional ingredients such as dried fruit or nuts can also add flavour, as well as texture and colour. Dried fruits are naturally sweet so you will need less sugar in cookies using these. When adding nuts, make sure they are really fresh.

Equipment

Most cookies can be made with nothing more sophisticated than weighing scales or measuring cups, a mixing bowl, fine sieve, rolling pin, wooden spoon, baking sheet and a wire rack for cooling.

ELECTRIC FOOD MIXERS AND PROCESSORS

These can be great time savers. Food mixers are good for creaming butter and sugar and beating in eggs, but you should still fold in dry ingredients by hand because it is easy to over-mix in a machine. Food processors are ideal for blending butter and sugar and are great for chopping or grinding nuts. A hand-held electric whisk is good for beating together ingredients and whisking egg whites. Choose one with three speeds and beaters that can be removed easily for cleaning.

BOWLS

You will need several bowls of different sizes, from large ones for mixing doughs to small, heatproof bowls in which to melt butter or chocolate.

BAKING SHEETS

Choose good quality, heavy baking sheets that won't buckle in high heat or develop hot-spots. Baking sheets are either entirely flat or have a lip along the length of one of the long sides; baking trays have a lip all round. Sheets are a better choice than trays because they allow air to circulate better within the oven.

BAKING TINS

Round or rectangular baking tins (pans) are used for brownies, bars and traybakes. The cookie mixture is pressed into the tin, then cut into squares or bars after baking. Tins with a dull finish will produce a crisper result than shiny ones.

WIRE RACKS

After baking, nearly all cookies must be transferred to a wire rack to cool. The rack allows air to circulate, which prevents the cookies from becoming soggy.

Left: A good selection of large and small heatproof bowls are very useful for cookie-making.

Above: Baking sheets are available in various sizes; some have a non-stick coating.

MEASURING SPOONS, JUGS AND CUPS

A set of measuring spoons is vital for measuring small quantities. For larger quantities, use a clearly marked jug (pitcher) or cup.

PASTRY BOARDS

These should be completely flat and smooth to allow cookie dough to be rolled out to an even thickness. They may be made of wood, marble or toughened glass.

Below: A set of measuring jugs and spoons are invaluable for measuring both wet and dry ingredients.

ROLLING PINS

Made of plastic, wood or marble, rolling pins are used for rolling out cookie dough or fondant icing for decorating cookies. They can also be used to crush ingredients such as cookies that are to be added to a no-bake cookie.

CUTTERS

Cookie cutters come in all shapes and sizes, from the simplest round cutters to families of gingerbread people, and are used to cut out shapes from rolled-out dough. For the best results the cutters should be metal and sharp.

PASTRY WHEELS

These can be used to cut rolled-out dough into squares, rectangles or diamonds quickly and simply.

COOKIE PRESSES

Similar in design and appearance to an icing syringe, cookie presses can be filled with a soft dough, which is then forced through a patterned disc to make pretty cookie shapes.

Above: Cookie cutters are available in all shapes and sizes, and also in sets.

PASTRY BRUSHES

These are useful for greasing baking sheets and glazing cookies. Brushes that have been used for glazing with beaten egg should be rinsed in cold water before being washed in hot soapy water. Rinse thoroughly, flick dry and leave to air.

SIEVES

If possible, have at least two sieves: a large one for sifting flour and a smaller one for dusting cookies with icing (confectioners') sugar.

WHISKS

A wire balloon whisk or hand-held rotary whisk is useful for whisking egg whites for cookie mixtures and whipping cream for cookie fillings.

SPATULAS

A flexible rubber or plastic spatula is useful for scraping cookie mixture from the bowl. It can also be used for folding in dry ingredients.

PALETTE KNIVES

Wide and round-bladed palette knives (metal spatulas) can be used for mixing liquid into cookie dough and for lifting cookies from baking sheets. Smaller ones can be used for spreading cookie fillings and icing.

Below: A piping bag can be used for shaping as well as decorating cookies.

PIPING BAGS AND NOZZLES

A medium to large piping (pastry) bag with a selection of plain and fluted nozzles is useful for both shaping and decorating cookies. Soft cookie dough can be piped through a large nozzle, while icing can be piped into delicate patterns through smaller nozzles.

TIMERS

These are available in various shapes and sizes and are essential for baking; just one minute can make the difference between a perfect cookie and an overbaked one.

Above:
Rolling pins are most commonly made of wood. Short rolling pins are also available and young children may find them easier to handle than longer ones.

Drop Cookies

This type of cookie is made from a soft, spoonable mixture that is dropped on to a baking sheet, then baked. The mixture is usually creamed and they are one of the simplest type of cookies to make.

CHOCOLATE CHIP COOKIES

These are a classic drop cookie. The basic recipe can be easily adapted to introduce other flavours.

Makes 12

115g/4oz/½ cup unsalted (sweet) butter, at room temperature, diced
115g/4oz/generous ½ cup caster (superfine) sugar
1 egg, lightly beaten
5ml/1 tsp vanilla essence (extract)
175g/6oz/1½ cups plain (all-purpose) flour
175g/6oz plain (semisweet) chocolate chips

1 Preheat the oven to 180°C/350°F/Gas 4. Lightly grease two large baking sheets.

2 Put the butter and sugar in a large bowl and beat together until pale and creamy. Beat in the egg and vanilla essence.

3 Sift the flour over the butter mixture and, using a large metal spoon, fold in the flour along with the chocolate chips.

4 Drop tablespoonfuls of the mixture on to the prepared baking sheets. (It should fall off the spoon quite easily with a sharp jerk.) Leave plenty of space between each one to allow for spreading during baking.

5 Flatten each cookie slightly with the back of a fork, keeping the shape of each one as even and round as possible.

6 Bake the cookies for about 10 minutes. Leave on the baking sheet for a few minutes to firm up, then transfer to a wire rack to cool.

Variations
Double choc Substitute 15ml/1 tbsp cocoa powder (unsweetened) for the same quantity of flour. For a chunkier texture, use roughly chopped chocolate instead of chocolate chips.
Macadamia nut or hazelnut Add whole or roughly chopped nuts instead of chocolate chips.

MELTED DROP COOKIES

Some drop cookies are made by the melting method, which involves melting butter and sugar or syrup to start the caramelization process before baking, then adding the flour and flavourings. The batter spreads considerably when heated, so always leave plenty of space between the cookies when dropping the batter on to the baking sheet.

SHAPING DROP COOKIES

Drop cookies made by the melting method are often extremely pliable when they first come out of the oven and can be shaped into curls, rolls and baskets. As they cool, the cookies harden and keep their shape.

Although shaping isn't difficult, timing is important. After taking the cookies out of the oven, they should be left on the baking sheet for about 15 seconds, then quickly removed with a palette knife (metal spatula) and moulded into shape.

To make curls or rolls, mould the cookie over a lightly oiled rolling pin or around a wooden spoon handle.

To make baskets, mould the cookie over an upturned ramekin or orange.

If the cookies have already hardened by the time you are ready to shape them, return them to the oven for a few seconds to soften.

Rolled Cookies

Cookie dough can be chilled, then rolled out and cut into shapes. To make perfect rolled cookies, the dough must be of the right consistency. If it is too dry, it will crack and crumble; if it is too wet the mixture may stick to the board and rolling pin and the cookies will spread during baking.

BASIC ROLLED COOKIES

This recipe uses a creamed dough, but cookie dough for rolling can also be made using the melting method or the rubbed-in method.

Makes 24

115g/4oz/½ cup unsalted (sweet) butter, at room temperature, diced
50g/2oz/¼ cup caster (superfine) sugar
1 egg, lightly beaten
15ml/1 tbsp finely ground almonds
200g/7oz/1¾ cups plain (all-purpose) flour
30ml/2 tbsp cornflour (cornstarch)

1 Put the butter and sugar in a large bowl and beat together until pale and creamy. Gradually add the egg, beating well after each addition, then beat in the ground almonds.

2 Sift the flour and cornflour over the butter and sugar mixture and stir to make a soft dough.

3 Turn the dough on to a lightly floured surface and knead until smooth. Shape into a ball, then flatten slightly. Wrap in clear film (plastic wrap) and chill for about 30 minutes, or until firm.

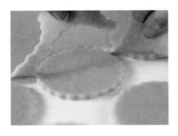

4 Preheat the oven to 180°C/350°F/ Gas 4. Lightly grease two or three large baking sheets.

5 Roll out the dough on a lightly floured surface to a thickness of about 3mm/⅛in. Cut or stamp out shapes, then re-roll the scraps to make more cookies.

6 Using a spatula, transfer the cookies to the prepared baking sheets, leaving a space of at least 2.5cm/1in between each.

7 Bake for 10 minutes, until pale golden brown. Leave the cookies on the baking sheets for 2–3 minutes, then transfer to a wire rack to cool.

CUTTING SHAPES

Rolled cookies can be cut into any shape or size. You can use a cookie cutter to stamp out shapes, or cut out shapes by hand.

USING A CUTTER Press the cutter firmly into the rolled out dough, then lift it off. Don't twist the cutter as this may distort the shape.

CUTTING BY HAND To make square, rectangular or triangular cookies, use a sharp knife or a pastry wheel and a ruler.

Trim the edges of the rolled dough to straighten them. To make rectangles, cut 4cm/1½in strips, then cut each strip at intervals of 5cm/2in. To make triangles, cut each square in half diagonally. To make diamond shapes, cut the dough into wide strips, then cut diagonally across the strips.

> ### MAKING A TEMPLATE
> To make unusual cookie shapes, you may need to make your own template. Avoid very intricate designs or ones with protrusions that could distort or burn during baking, or break off easily.
>
> Draw the design on a piece of thin card and cut out. Alternatively, trace the shape on a piece of greaseproof (waxed) paper, then stick it on to card and cut it out.
>
> Place the template on the rolled out dough and cut around it with the point of a knife. Transfer the cookie to the baking sheet, taking care not to distort the shape.

Piped Cookies

The cookie dough for piping needs to be soft enough to squeeze through a piping (pastry) bag but firm enough to keep its shape during baking. Creamed mixtures are usually used, producing a cookie with a crumbly, airy texture.

BASIC PIPED COOKIES

Piping cookie dough requires a certain amount of dexterity so may be too difficult for young children to attempt. If they want to have a go, use a soft, meringue-based mixture rather than a creamed one.

Makes 12–16
175g/6oz/¾ cup unsalted (sweet)
   butter, at room temperature, diced
40g/1½ oz/3 tbsp icing (confectioners')
   sugar, sifted
2.5ml/½ tsp vanilla essence (extract)
175g/6oz/1½ cups plain
   (all-purpose) flour
40g/1½ oz/3 tbsp cornflour (cornstarch)

1 Preheat the oven to 180°C/350°F/ Gas 4. Grease four baking sheets.

2 Cream the butter and sugar together in a bowl until very pale and fluffy. Beat in the vanilla essence.

3 Sift the flour and cornflour over the butter mixture and mix together until smooth.

4 Spoon the mixture into a piping bag with a 12mm/½in star nozzle.

5 Pipe rosettes about 5cm/2in across on the baking sheets, spacing well apart. Bake for 12–15 minutes, until pale golden. Leave the cookies on the baking sheets for a few minutes, then transfer to a wire rack.

PIPING DIFFERENT SHAPES

The basic mixture can be piped into long finger shapes or swirls.

To make long fingers, pipe 6cm/2¼in lengths of dough on to baking sheets, spacing them well apart.

To make two tone swirls, divide the mixture between two bowls and beat 15ml/1 tbsp sifted cocoa powder (unsweetened) into one bowl. Spoon plain mixture into the piping bag down one side and chocolate mixture down the other. Pipe swirls into 12 paper cake cases.

PERFECT PIPING
• Use a strong piping bag.
• Drop the nozzle into the bag and push down so that it fits firmly. Rotate the end of the bag so that there is a twist just above the nozzle, closing it off while you fill the bag.
• Fold the top of the bag over your hand to make a "collar". Spoon in some mixture until the bag is only half full, then gently twist the top of the bag. Push down with your fingers so that the dough pushes into the nozzle.
• Hold the twisted end of the bag in one hand; use the other to guide the nozzle. Use a firm, steady pressure. As soon as the shape is complete, stop applying pressure, push down slightly, then lift the nozzle away.

Shaped Cookies

Cookie dough can be moulded into various shapes and sizes. Simple shapes can be formed by hand, while more intricate shapes can be made using a cookie press.

FORK COOKIES

These are the very simplest hand-moulded cookies. Pieces of dough are rolled into balls, then flattened using the back of a fork.

Makes 16

115g/4oz/½ cup unsalted (sweet) butter, at room temperature, diced
50g/2oz/¼ cup caster (superfine) sugar
150g/5oz/1¼ cups self-raising (self-rising) flour, sifted

I Preheat the oven to 180°C/350°F/Gas 4. Lightly grease two baking sheets or line with baking parchment. Put the butter in a bowl and beat until creamy, then beat in the sugar. Stir in the flour to form a dough.

2 Shape the dough into walnut-size balls and place on the baking sheets, spacing them well apart. Dip a fork in cold water, then press down once on each cookie to flatten.

3 Bake for 10–12 minutes until pale brown. Leave on the baking sheets for a few minutes, then transfer to a wire rack to cool completely.

PRESSED COOKIES

A commercial-style cookie press can make quick work of moulding cookie dough. The dough needs to be very smooth to go through the fine holes in the cookie discs, so a press is no good for chunky doughs containing other ingredients such as chopped nuts or chocolate chips. If the cookie dough is too firm to push through the press, add a few more drops of milk; if it is slightly soft and sticks to the cookie disc, chill it briefly.

Makes 25 x 5cm/2in cookies

90g/3½oz/7 tbsp unsalted (sweet) butter, at room temperature, diced
90g/3½oz/½ cup caster (superfine) sugar
1 egg yolk
165g/5½oz/scant 1½ cups plain (all-purpose) flour
5ml/1 tsp vanilla essence (extract)
5ml/1 tsp milk
sugar or nuts, to decorate (optional)

I Grease two baking sheets. Beat together the butter and sugar until pale, then beat in the egg yolk.

2 Sift the flour over the mixture and add the vanilla essence and milk. Fold together to make a soft dough.

3 Turn out the dough on to a lightly floured surface and then knead very briefly until smooth.

4 Following the instructions for your cookie press, attach a suitable disc, then fill the cylinder almost to the top with the dough you have made. Screw the plunger on to the cookie press, then press the dough on to the baking sheets, spacing the cookies slightly apart.

5 Put the baking sheets in the refrigerator and chill the cookies for at least 30 minutes, so that they will keep their shape during baking. Meanwhile, preheat the oven to 180°C/350°F/Gas 4.

6 Sprinkle sugar or nuts over the cookies, if you decide to use them, then bake for about 15 minutes, or until the cookies are very lightly browned.

7 Leave the cookies on the baking sheets for about 5 minutes so that they firm up slightly, then you can them transfer to a wire rack to cool completely.

Bar Cookies

These are baked in a tray, then cut into bars or squares and can vary greatly. Some are thin and crunchy, others are thick and chewy while some are light and spongy.

FRUIT AND NUT BARS

This layered bar cookie consists of a shortbread-style base, a fruity filling and an almond cookie topping.

Makes 15

250g/9oz/2¼ cups plain (all-purpose) flour, sifted
175g/6oz/¾ cup chilled butter, diced
75g/3oz/scant ½ cup caster (superfine) sugar
icing (confectioners') sugar, for dusting

FOR THE FILLING

115g/4oz/½ cup glacé (candied) cherries, roughly chopped
50g/2oz/⅓ cup sultanas (golden raisins)
50g/2oz/½ cup almonds, roughly chopped

FOR THE TOPPING

115g/4oz/½ cup butter, at room temperature, diced
115g/4oz/generous ½ cup caster (superfine) sugar or soft brown sugar
2 eggs
50g/2oz/½ cup plain (all-purpose) flour
50g/2oz/½ cup ground almonds

1 Preheat the oven to 180°C/350°F/ Gas 4. Grease and line a 18 × 28 × 2.5cm/7 × 11 × 1in cake tin (pan) with baking parchment.

2 Put the flour and butter into a bowl and rub together until the mixture resembles breadcrumbs. Add the sugar and mix in with your hands until the dough starts to come together.

3 Press the mixture into the tin and level the surface. Prick with a fork, then bake for 10 minutes.

4 Remove the tin from the oven and reduce the oven temperature to 160°C/325°F/Gas 3. Combine the filling ingredients and sprinkle evenly over the baked base.

5 To make the topping, cream the butter and sugar until pale and fluffy, then beat in the eggs. Sift over the flour and fold in with the ground almonds, then spread over the fruit and nuts.

6 Bake for 30 minutes, or until golden and firm to the touch. Check the topping is cooked by inserting a wooden cocktail stick (toothpick); it should come out clean.

7 Leave to cool for 15 minutes, then dust with icing sugar and cut into squares or fingers.

BROWNIES

These classic bar cookies are moist and chewy, with a sugary crust.

Makes 24

225g/8oz plain (semisweet) chocolate
225g/8oz/1 cup unsalted (sweet) butter
3 eggs
225g/8oz/1 cup caster (superfine) sugar
30ml/2 tbsp strong black coffee
75g/3oz/⅔ cup self-raising (self-rising) flour
pinch of salt
150g/5oz/1¼ cups chopped walnuts
5ml/1 tsp vanilla essence (extract)

1 Preheat the oven to 190°C/375°F/ Gas 5. Grease and line an 18 × 28cm/ 7 × 11in tin (pan). Melt the chocolate and butter in a bowl set over a pan of simmering water. Leave to cool for 5 minutes.

2 In a large bowl, beat together the eggs, sugar and coffee, then beat in the melted chocolate. Sift the flour over the mixture, add the salt and fold in with the walnuts and vanilla.

3 Pour the mixture into the tin and bake for 35–40 minutes, or until just firm to the touch in the centre. (It will firm up as it cools.)

4 Leave to cool in the tin, then turn out on to a board, trim off the crusty edges and cut into squares.

Baking and Storing Cookies

Care must be taken when baking cookies. Always preheat the oven. It will take about 15 minutes to reach the required temperature, slightly less if the oven is fan-assisted. Cookies should usually be baked on the middle shelf or just above the middle of the oven.

Before you start, make sure the baking sheets fit the oven. There should be a small gap at either side and at the back of each baking sheet to allow hot air to circulate.

If you need to divide the cookies between two or more baking sheets, do this equally. If you are baking several sheets of cookies, don't put more than two sheets in the oven at a time or the temperature may drop. Switch the baking sheets round halfway through cooking. If you need to reuse the baking sheets for more cookies, let them cool before adding more cookies, otherwise the residual heat will make the second batch of cookies spread too much.

BAKING TIMES

Depending on the efficiency of your oven and whether the dough has been chilled, you may need to make small adjustments to baking times. Check cookies 2–3 minutes before the end of the suggested cooking time; unlike cakes they will not sink if the oven door is opened. However, don't do this too often or the oven temperature will drop.

Once the oven has heated up, subsequent batches of cookies may take less time to bake. Cookies tend to continue cooking for a minute or two after removing from the oven, so take this into account when judging whether they are done.

STORING COOKIES

With few exceptions, cookies are best eaten on the day that they are made. Some, such as American-style soft cookies, are at their most delicious when still slightly warm from the oven, but most cookies need to be cooled to allow them to crisp.

If you're not planning to eat the cookies straight away, store them as soon as they have cooled. Store crisp and soft cookies separately.

Store soft cookies in an airtight container. Ideally, they should also be stored in the refrigerator. To restore any that have hardened, add a slice of brown bread to the container. Replace the bread daily.

Crisp cookies do not need to be stored in an absolutely airtight container. Ceramic containers and glass jars with cork stoppers are ideal. Before adding the cookies, place a little crumpled tissue paper on the base to absorb any moisture.

In humid conditions, crisp cookies can become soft if not stored in an airtight container. To re-crisp cookies, place them on a baking sheet and put them in a preheated oven at 150°C/300°F/Gas 2 for 3 minutes. Cool on a wire rack before storing.

STORING UNBAKED COOKIE DOUGH

Providing cookie dough does not contain self-raising (self-rising) flour or a raising agent, it can be stored in the refrigerator or frozen. Cookie dough can be stored in the refrigerator overnight; dough for refrigerator cookies can be stored for up to a week; both can be frozen for up to three months.

To store in the refrigerator, wrap the dough in clear film (plastic wrap) to prevent it drying out. To freeze dough, double wrap in clear film.

To freeze unbaked cookies, open-freeze them on baking sheets, then pack into airtight containers, interleaving the layers with baking parchment. Thaw the cookies on baking sheets before baking.

Decorating Cookies

Cookies can be decorated before or after baking, when the cookies are still warm or after they have cooled.

ADDING TOPPINGS BEFORE BAKING

Many cookies are decorated before they are baked. They can be sprinkled with a little sugar or chopped nuts, for example, or can be brushed with a glossy glaze. Pretty patterns can be painted on to unbaked cookies with edible food colouring.

SUGAR

A crunchy sugar topping is one of the easiest and most effective ways to decorate cookies. When added before baking, the sugar sticks to the surface of the dough, and bakes to a glistening finish.

Dust unbaked cookies with a little icing (confectioners') sugar. Alternatively, to make a crunchy topping, sprinkle with a coarse sugar such as granulated or demerara.

NUTS

Cookies topped with nuts look very pretty. Nuts brown during baking, so don't put them on cookies that are baked for a long time or at a high temperature. (Be cautious about using nuts on cookies for young children.)

Gently press a whole or halved nut on top of unbaked cookies. Alternatively, sprinkle cookies with chopped or flaked (sliced) nuts.

GLAZES

These can provide a surface for toppings such as sugar or nuts to stick to, or they can simply give a glossy finish to the baked cookies. Beaten egg is the most common glaze used for cookies.

Egg or egg yolk gives a rich, glossy finish. Use a whole beaten egg or egg yolk. Dilute the egg with 15ml/ 1 tbsp cold water or milk, and add a pinch of caster (superfine) sugar, if you like. The glaze should be brushed on the cookies just before baking.

Brushing cookies with lightly beaten egg white produces a clear, shiny finish. It is best to brush the egg white on the cookies halfway through baking time.

Edible food colouring can be used to colour glazes. Beat an egg yolk and divide it among several small dishes. Mix one or two drops of food colouring into each one (the yellow of the yolk may alter certain colours). Using a fine brush paint patterns on to the cookies. Allow to dry slightly before baking.

ADDING TOPPINGS AND FILLINGS AFTER BAKING

Topping and filling simple cookies with icing can make them really special. Once iced, eat within 4 days.

GLACE ICING

This is perfect for drizzling over cookies or piping simple designs.

Sufficient to top 24 cookies
115g/4oz/1 cup icing
   (confectioners') sugar
a few drops of vanilla essence (extract)
15ml/1 tbsp hot water
a few drops of food colouring (optional)

1 Sift the icing sugar into a bowl, then add the vanilla essence. Gradually stir in the hot water until the mixture is the consistency of thick cream. Stir in a few drops of food colouring, if using.

2 Spoon a little icing into the centre of each cookie and spread out to the edges. Leave to dry for 1–2 minutes.

BUTTERCREAM

This smooth, creamy icing can be used to sandwich cookies together. It is also good for piping over cookies or as a simple cookie topping.

Sandwiches 12–14 pairs of cookies
50g/2oz/¼ cup softened unsalted (sweet)
   butter, at room temperature, diced
90g/3½oz/scant 1 cup icing
   (confectioners') sugar
5ml/1 tsp vanilla essence (extract)

1 Beat the butter until smooth and creamy, then gradually beat in the icing sugar and vanilla essence.

2 To fill cookies, spread a little buttercream on to the top of a cookie, then place a second cookie on top and gently press together.

Variation
To make chocolate buttercream, combine 10ml/2 tsp cocoa powder (unsweetened) with 20ml/4 tsp boiling water. Leave to cool, then beat into the buttercream.

READY-TO-ROLL ICING

Available in most supermarkets, this smooth ready-made icing is great for decorating cookies.

Roll out the icing thinly and cut into shapes. Press the shapes on to rolled cookies. Alternatively, melt the icing to make a smooth spreadable topping.

CHOCOLATE TOPPINGS
Melted chocolate is a good alternative to icing. The simplest way to coat cookies in chocolate is to lay them on a wire rack with a sheet of greaseproof (waxed) paper underneath the rack.

Spoon melted chocolate over the cookies (any excess will drip on to the paper). Leave to set. Unless it is very warm, don't chill chocolate-coated cookies as the chocolate will lose its glossy appearance.

MAKING PATTERNS

Creating decorative patterns on cookies is great fun. Stunning designs can be achieved with very little effort or skill, and even quite young children can join in and help.

USING A STENCIL

No decoration could be quicker or easier than dusting freshly baked cookies with icing (confectioners') sugar or a little cocoa powder (unsweetened). You can buy special stencils made for cookie decorating or you can make your own by drawing a simple design on thin cardboard and cutting it out.

Place a stencil on the cookie. Using a fine sieve, dredge with sugar or cocoa, then carefully lift off the stencil to reveal the design.

For a really simple design, dust a cookie with sugar, then cover half with a piece of cardboard and dust the other half with cocoa powder.

PATTERNED ICING

Piping patterns on cookies can be time-consuming and requires a certain amount of skill. However, with very little effort, you can create stunning patterns with contrasting colours of glacé (candied) icing.

To make a feathered design, spread a cookie with glacé icing. Leave it to set slightly, then pipe straight parallel lines of icing in a contrasting colour across the top of the cookie. Draw a wooden cocktail stick (toothpick) through the lines at a 90-degree angle.

To make a cobweb design, spread a cookie with glacé icing. Leave it to set slightly, then pipe concentric circles of icing in a contrasting colour on to the cookie. Draw a wooden cocktail stick (toothpick) across the cookie from the centre outwards, dividing the design into quarters, then draw the skewer from the edge of the cookie inwards, dividing it into eighths.

WRITING AND DRAWING

Tubes of writing icing are handy for writing simple messages and drawing lines, swirls and dots. For best results, gently knead the icing in the tube before opening it to make it pliable for piping. Some tubes come with interchangeable nozzles, so that you can pipe tiny rosettes and scrolls as well.

Food colouring pens look like felt-tipped pens but are filled with edible food colouring. They are great for writing names or creating simple designs on plain or iced cookies.

DRIZZLING WITH CHOCOLATE

Thin lines of chocolate can be drizzled over cookies to make attractive patterns. You can drizzle chocolate from a spoon or, for finer lines, you can pipe the chocolate.

To pipe lines of melted chocolate, use a paper piping (pastry) bag and snip off the merest tip.

Cookie Gifts

Cookies make a great gift and kids really enjoy getting involved in making, baking, decorating and wrapping them. Leave gift wrapping until the last minute, so the cookies are as fresh as possible. It is also a good idea to include information about the ingredients, particularly if the cookies contain nuts.

BOXES, TINS AND JARS

Packaging cookies in attractive containers is one of the simplest ways to make an appealing gift.

Airtight containers such as glass storage jars or tins are practical because they will keep the cookies fresh and can be used again and again. You can buy very decorative jars and tins in kitchenware stores, which make lovely gifts.

Stationers and department stores sell beautiful gift boxes in all shapes and sizes, patterns and colours, which look stunning tied with ribbon. Shallow boxes that hold the cookies in one or just a few layers are best, particularly if the cookies are fragile or have been decorated with delicate icing.

When packing cookies in a gift box, line the box with greaseproof (waxed) paper or crumpled tissue paper to protect the cookies, then fill with cookies.

NOVELTY CONTAINERS

It can be fun to pack cookies inside containers other than the classic box or jar. A pretty mug or bowl makes an ideal container for cookies, and creates two gifts in one.

Wrap the cookies in clear, coloured or patterned cellophane to keep them fresh, then put the package inside a colourful cup or bowl.

BAGS

You can buy ready-made bags from card stores and stationers, but it's fun and simple to make cookie bags with clear or coloured cellophane. These little packages look particularly pretty tied with coloured ribbon.

To make a simple sack-shaped bag, which is suitable for round or square cookies, cut a 25cm/10in square of cellophane. Put a pile of six cookies in the middle of the square. Gather up the edges around the cookies, then tie with ribbon.

To make a pointed bag for finger-shaped or tiny cookies, cut out a 40cm/16in square of cellophane. Fold in quarters to make a smaller square. Holding the square where the folds join, cut across the opposite corner in a curved line. Open into a circle, then cut in half to make two semicircles. Take one semicircle and pull its two points towards each other until they meet. Slide one of the points behind the other to make a cone. Secure with sticky tape. Half-fill with cookies, then gather and tie with ribbon.

Cylindrical cookies can be wrapped to look like crackers. Roll in a rectangle of cellophane, then tie both ends with ribbon.

GIFT TAGS

A small label adds the final touch to your gift-wrapped cookies. Buy or make one to co-ordinate with your chosen box or container.

Teatime Treats

There's nothing quite like coming home from school to a plate of freshly baked cookies and a glass of milk. This chapter is packed with lots of delightful ideas that kids will love to eat, from simple cookies with pretty sugar icing to utterly adorable puppy faces and indulgent ice-cream sandwiches.

Jammie Sweethearts

These buttery cookies are an absolute classic. Sandwiched with buttercream and a generous dollop of strawberry jam, they make a perfect snack served with a glass of milk at teatime, or are equally good wrapped tightly, and popped in a lunch box as a post-sandwich treat.

Makes 20
225g/8oz/2 cups plain (all-purpose) flour
175g/6oz/¾ cup unsalted (sweet) butter,
  chilled and diced
130g/4¼oz/⅔ cup caster
  (superfine) sugar
1 egg yolk

FOR THE FILLING
50g/2oz/¼ cup unsalted (sweet)
  butter, at room temperature, diced
90g/3½oz/scant 1 cup icing
  (confectioners') sugar
60–75ml/4–5 tbsp strawberry jam

Cook's Tip
If you don't have a small cutter for the cookie centres, use a sharp knife to cut out triangles or squares instead.

1 Put the flour and butter in a food processor and process until the mixture resembles breadcrumbs. Add the sugar and egg yolk and process until the mixture starts to form a dough.

2 Turn out on to a floured surface and knead until smooth. Shape into a ball, wrap in clear film (plastic wrap) and chill for at least 30 minutes. Preheat the oven to 180°C/350°F/ Gas 4. Grease two baking sheets.

3 Roll out the dough thinly on a lightly floured surface and cut out rounds using a 6cm/2½in cookie cutter. Re-roll the trimmings and cut out more rounds until you have 40.

4 Place half the cookie rounds on a prepared baking sheet. Using a small heart-shaped cutter, about 2cm/¾in in diameter, cut out the centres of the remaining rounds. Place on the second baking sheet.

5 Bake the cookies for about 12 minutes until pale golden, then transfer to a wire rack and leave to cool completely.

6 To make the buttercream, beat together the butter and sugar until smooth and creamy.

7 Using a palette knife (metal spatula), spread a little buttercream on to each cookie round. Spoon a little jam on to the buttercream, then gently press the cut out cookies on top, so that the jam fills the heart-shaped hole.

Peanut Crunch Cookies

These delicious sweet and nutty cookies are so easy to make. They puff up into lovely domed rounds during baking, giving them a really professional look. If you prefer cookies with a slightly less nutty texture, use smooth peanut butter rather than the crunchy variety.

Makes 25

115g/4oz/½ cup unsalted (sweet)
  butter, at room temperature, diced
115g/4oz/generous ½ cup light
  muscovado (brown) sugar
1 egg
150g/5oz/1¼ cups self-raising
  (self-rising) flour
2.5ml/½ tsp baking powder
150g/5oz/generous ½ cup crunchy
  peanut butter
icing (confectioners') sugar, for dusting

1 Preheat the oven to 190°C/375°F/
Gas 5. Grease two baking sheets.

2 Put the butter and sugar in a mixing bowl and beat until pale and creamy. Beat in the egg, then add the flour, baking powder and peanut butter. Beat until the ingredients are thoroughly mixed.

3 Place heaped teaspoonfuls of the mixture on to the greased baking sheets; space well apart to allow the cookies to spread while baking. (If necessary, spoon the dough on to the baking sheets in batches.)

4 Bake the cookies for about 20 minutes until risen; they will still be quite soft to the touch.

5 Leave the cookies on the baking sheets for about 5 minutes, then transfer to a wire rack to cool. To serve, lightly dust with icing sugar.

Pink Sugared Hearts

Pretty and pink, these delightful cookies are always a hit with Barbie-loving girls. Rolling the edges of the cookies in coloured sugar to accentuate their shape really adds to the fun of decorating.

Makes 32
225g/8oz/2 cups plain
  (all-purpose) flour
175g/6oz/¾ cup unsalted (sweet)
  butter, chilled and diced
130g/4¼oz/⅔ cup caster
  (superfine) sugar
1 egg yolk

For the decoration
50g/2oz/¼ cup granulated sugar
pink food colouring
225g/8oz/2 cups icing
  (confectioners') sugar
30–45ml/2–3 tbsp lemon juice

1 Put the flour and butter into a food processor, then process in short bursts until the mixture resembles fine breadcrumbs. Add the sugar and egg yolk to the food processor and process until the mixture just begins to form a ball.

2 Turn the dough out on to a lightly floured surface and knead until smooth. Shape the dough into a ball, wrap in clear film (plastic wrap) and chill in the refrigerator for at least 30 minutes.

3 Preheat the oven to 180°C/350°F/Gas 4. Grease two baking sheets.

4 Working in batches, roll out the dough thinly on a lightly floured surface and cut out heart shapes using a 5cm/2in cutter. Transfer to the baking sheets, spacing them slightly apart. Bake for 10 minutes, or until pale golden. Transfer to a wire rack to cool.

5 To decorate, put the granulated sugar in a bowl and add a small dot of pink food colouring. Using the back of a teaspoon, work the food colouring into the sugar until completely pink.

6 Put the icing sugar in a separate bowl and add 30ml/2 tbsp of the lemon juice, stirring until smooth but spreadable. If the paste is too thick add a little more lemon juice and stir until well combined.

Cook's Tip
To make festive cookies try cutting out tree shapes and use green food colouring instead of pink. Alternatively, cut out star shapes and use silver or gold food colouring to tint the sugar. Children will love these festive shapes and will enjoy leaving a plate of cookies and a glass of milk out for Santa.

7 Using a palette knife (metal spatula) spread a little icing on to each cookie, to within 5mm/¼in of the edge.

8 Turn each iced cookie on its side and gently turn in the coloured sugar so that the edges of the icing become coated in pink sugar. Leave the cookies to set for about 1 hour.

Butter Gems

These tiny shortbread-based cookies are topped with rosettes of soft buttercream and a pretty sprinkling of brightly coloured sugar. They make a lovely treat for even the smallest of mouths.

Makes about 40

115g/4oz/½ cup unsalted (sweet)
  butter, at room temperature, diced
50g/2oz/¼ cup caster (superfine) sugar
175g/6oz/1½ cups plain
  (all-purpose) flour

FOR THE DECORATION

50g/2oz/4 tbsp unsalted (sweet) butter,
  at room temperature, diced
5ml/1 tsp vanilla essence (extract)
90g/3½ oz/scant 1 cup icing
  (confectioners') sugar
25g/1oz/2 tbsp granulated sugar
green, lilac or pink food colourings

1 Put the butter and the sugar in a large bowl and beat together until smooth and creamy. Add the flour to the creamed butter and then mix well to form a thick paste.

2 Turn the dough on to a lightly floured surface and knead until smooth. Wrap the dough in clear film (plastic wrap) and chill in the refrigerator for at least 30 minutes.

3 Preheat the oven to 180°C/350°F/ Gas 4. Grease two baking sheets.

4 Roll out the dough on a lightly floured surface and cut out rounds using a 3.5cm/1¼in cookie cutter. Space slightly apart on the baking sheets and bake for 10 minutes, or until pale golden. Transfer to a wire rack to cool completely.

5 To decorate the cookies, beat the butter with the vanilla essence and icing sugar until smooth and creamy. Spoon the buttercream into a piping (pastry) bag fitted with a star-shaped nozzle, then pipe a rosette on to each cookie.

6 Put the granulated sugar into a small bowl and add several drops of the food colouring. Using the back of a teaspoon work the colouring into the sugar until it is deeply coloured. Sprinkle a little of the sugar over the cookies.

Alphabetinis

These funny little letters are great for kids – and might even be a good way to encourage them to practise their spelling. They are great fun to make and even better to eat.

Makes about 30

2 egg whites
15ml/1 tbsp cornflour (cornstarch)
50g/2oz/½ cup plain (all-purpose) flour
150g/5oz/¾ cup caster (superfine) sugar
10ml/2 tsp vanilla essence (extract)
90g/3½oz milk chocolate

1 Preheat the oven to 180°C/350°F/Gas 4. Line two large baking sheets with baking parchment.

2 In a clean glass bowl, whisk the egg whites until peaking. Sift the cornflour and plain flour over the egg whites and add the sugar and vanilla essence. Fold in using a large metal spoon.

3 Spoon half the mixture into a plastic bag and gently squeeze it into a corner of the bag. Snip off the tip of the corner so that the cookie mixture can be squeezed out in a thin line, 1cm/½in wide.

4 Very carefully, pipe letters on to one of the lined baking sheets, making each letter about 6cm/2½in tall. Spoon the remaining cookie mixture into the bag and pipe more letters on to the second lined baking sheet.

5 Bake the cookies for 12 minutes, or until crisp and golden. Carefully transfer to a wire rack to cool.

6 Break the chocolate into pieces and put in a heatproof bowl set over a pan of simmering water. Heat, stirring frequently, until melted.

7 Spoon the melted chocolate into a small paper piping (pastry) bag (or use a smaller plastic bag) and snip off the merest tip.

8 Pipe the chocolate in lines over the cookies to highlight the shape of each letter. Leave to set for at least 1 hour.

Flower Power Cookies

Look out for little piped sugar flower decorations in the supermarket. Some are in delicate, pale colours, while others are much brighter and more vibrant. The latter are best for these colourful cookies as they contrast better with the pretty pastel-coloured icing.

Makes 28

225g/8oz/2 cups plain (all-purpose) flour
175g/6oz/¾ cup unsalted (sweet)
   butter, chilled and diced
finely grated rind of 1 orange
130g/4¼oz/⅔ cup light muscovado
   (brown) sugar
1 egg yolk

FOR THE DECORATION

30ml/2 tbsp orange juice
200g/7oz/1¾ cups icing
   (confectioners') sugar
green, yellow and orange food colourings
multi-coloured sugared flowers, to decorate

1 Put the flour, butter and orange rind into a food processor. Process until the mixture resembles fine breadcrumbs. Add the sugar and egg yolk to the food processor and process until the mixture starts to bind together.

2 Turn the mixture out on to a lightly floured surface and knead until it forms a dough. Shape the dough into a ball and wrap tightly in clear film (plastic wrap) and chill in the refrigerator for at least 30 minutes.

3 Preheat the oven to 180°C/350°F/ Gas 4. Grease two baking sheets. Roll out the dough thinly on a floured surface and cut out rounds using a fluted cookie cutter about 6cm/2½in in diameter.

4 Transfer the cookies to the baking sheets, spacing them slightly apart. Bake for 12–15 minutes until pale golden, then transfer to a wire rack to cool completely.

5 To decorate the cookies, put the orange juice in a bowl and gradually stir in the icing sugar until the mixture has the consistency of thick pouring cream. Divide the mixture among three bowls and stir a few drops of a different food colouring into each bowl.

6 Spoon a little green icing on to one third of the cookies, spreading it to within 1cm/½in of the cookie edges. Top each one with a sugared flower (ideally of a contrasting colour). Decorate the remaining cookies in the same way, using the yellow icing on half the cookies and the orange icing on the remaining half. Leave to set for about 1 hour.

Dolly Cookies

These cute cookies look like they belong at a doll's tea party and are easy for kids to make and decorate. The cookies are made by simply chilling a roll of dough, then slicing off pieces on to a baking sheet, so you don't even need cookie cutters. Baking doesn't get much easier than this.

Makes 14

115g/4oz/½ cup unsalted (sweet)
   butter, at room temperature, diced
50g/2oz/¼ cup caster
   (superfine) sugar
pink food colouring
5ml/1 tsp vanilla essence (extract)
175g/6oz/1½ cups plain
   (all-purpose) flour
90g/3½oz white chocolate
75g/3oz multi-coloured
   sweets (candies)

1 Put the butter and sugar in a bowl with a dash of pink food colouring and the vanilla essence. Beat together until smooth and creamy.

2 Add the flour to the butter and sugar mixture and stir well until thoroughly combined. Turn the dough out on to a lightly floured surface and knead until smooth.

3 Using your hands, roll the dough into a thick sausage shape, about 12cm/4½in long and 5cm/2in in diameter. Wrap the dough in clear film (plastic wrap) and chill in the refrigerator for at least 30 minutes.

4 Preheat the oven to 180°C/350°F/ Gas 4. Grease two large baking sheets.

5 Cut the dough into 5mm/¼in slices and space them slightly apart on the baking sheets. Bake for 15–18 minutes, or until the cookies begin to colour. Transfer to a wire rack to cool completely.

6 Break the chocolate into pieces and put in a heatproof bowl set over a pan of simmering water. Heat, stirring frequently, until the chocolate has melted. Using a sharp knife, cut the sweets in half.

7 Using a small palette knife (metal spatula) swirl a little chocolate on to each cookie and decorate with a ring of sweets. Leave to set.

Gingerbread Family

You can have great fun with these cookies by creating characters with different features. By using an assortment of different gingerbread cutters you can make a gingerbread family of all shapes and sizes. If you want to make decorating the cookies simpler, use just one colour of chocolate rather than three. Coloured writer icing and candy are also good for decorating.

Makes about 12

*350g/12oz/3 cups plain
   (all-purpose) flour*
*5ml/1 tsp bicarbonate of soda
   (baking soda)*
5ml/1 tsp ground ginger
*115g/4oz/½ cup unsalted (sweet)
   butter, chilled and diced*
*175/6oz/scant 1 cup light muscovado
   (brown) sugar*
1 egg
*30ml/2 tbsp black treacle (molasses)
   or golden (light corn) syrup*
*50g/2oz each plain, milk and white
   chocolate, to decorate*

1 Preheat the oven to 180°C/ 350°F/Gas 4. Grease two or three large baking sheets.

2 Put the flour, bicarbonate of soda, ginger and diced butter into the bowl of the food processor. Process until the mixture begins to resemble fine breadcrumbs.

3 If necessary, scrape down the sides of the food processor bowl with a wooden spoon or spatula to remove any crumbs that have become stuck to the sides.

4 Add the sugar, egg and black treacle or golden syrup to the food processor and process the mixture until it begins to form into a ball.

5 Turn the dough out on to a lightly floured surface, and knead until it is smooth and pliable.

6 Roll out the dough on a lightly floured surface (you might find it easier to roll half of the dough out at a time). Cut out figures using people-shaped cutters, then transfer to the baking sheets. Re-roll any trimmings and cut out more figures.

7 Bake for 15 minutes until slightly risen and starting to colour around the edges. Leave for 5 minutes, then transfer to a wire rack to cool.

8 To decorate the cookies, break each type of chocolate into a separate bowl. One at a time, set a bowl over a pan of simmering water and heat, stirring frequently, until melted. Spoon the melted chocolate into paper piping (pastry) bags, snip off the merest tip, then pipe faces and clothes on to the cookies. Leave to set.

Cook's Tip
You can use any colour of sugar for these cookies: the darker the sugar, the darker the final cookies will be. Similarly, if you use black treacle rather than golden syrup the cookies will be darker.

Puppy Faces

Children of any age can have fun making these little pups – you could even use the family pet as a model. The cookies are decorated with the widely available, white ready-to-roll icing, but you can knead in a little black, brown or yellow food colouring to make different-coloured dogs.

Makes 10

100g/3½oz/scant 1 cup plain
(all-purpose) flour
50g/2oz/½ cup rolled oats
2.5ml/½ tsp mixed spice (apple pie spice)
50g/2oz/¼ cup unsalted (sweet) butter,
chilled and diced
100g/3½oz/½ cup caster
(superfine) sugar
1 egg yolk

FOR THE DECORATION

60ml/4 tbsp apricot jam
250g/9oz white ready-to-roll icing
10 round coloured sweets (candies)
black and red writer icing tubes
icing (confectioners') sugar, for dusting

1 Put the flour, rolled oats, mixed spice and butter into the food processor. Process until the mixture resembles fine breadcrumbs.

2 Add the sugar, egg yolk and 5ml/1 tsp water to the food processor and blend until the mixture begins to form a ball.

3 Turn the dough out on to a lightly floured surface and knead until smooth. Wrap in clear film (plastic wrap) and chill for 30 minutes.

4 Preheat the oven to 200°C/400°F/Gas 6. Grease a large baking sheet.

5 Roll out the dough on a floured surface and cut out rounds using a 6cm/2½in cutter. Transfer to the baking sheet, spacing slightly apart. Bake for 12 minutes until pale golden. Transfer to a wire rack to cool.

6 Press the jam through a sieve. Brush a little jam over each cookie to within 5mm/¼in of the edge.

7 Roll out half the icing as thinly as possible on a surface dusted with icing sugar. Cut out 10 rounds using the 6cm/2½in cutter and lay one over each cookie. To make the eyes, halve the coloured sweets, brush the icing lightly with water and press the sweets into the cookies.

8 Use the black writer tube to pipe the noses and mouths, finishing with a little red tongue.

9 To make the ears, divide the remaining icing into 20 pieces. Roll each piece into a ball and flatten between the thumb and forefinger to make a flat pear shape. Lightly brush the icing with water and secure the ears. Arrange the cookies in a single layer on a tray.

Tree Cookies

These cookies look really effective with their chocolate-finger cookie trunks and brightly coloured "fruits". Kids will love helping to decorate them. Arrange the cookies in a line on the tea table (preferably on a multi-coloured cloth if you have one).

Makes 10

50g/2oz/ ¼ cup unsalted (sweet) butter,
* at room temperature, diced*
115g/4oz/ ½ cup light muscovado
* (brown) sugar*
1 egg
150g/5oz/1¼ cups self-raising
* (self-rising) flour*
2.5ml/½ tsp bicarbonate of soda
* (baking soda)*
finely grated rind of 1 lemon

FOR THE DECORATION
50g/2oz/½ cup icing
* (confectioners') sugar*
10ml/2 tsp lemon juice
10 milk chocolate fingers
brightly coloured sweets (candies),
* such as m&ms*

1 Preheat the oven to 180°C/350°F/ Gas 4. Grease two baking sheets.

2 In a large bowl, beat together the butter and sugar until smooth and creamy. Beat in the egg. Add the flour, bicarbonate of soda and lemon rind and mix until smooth.

3 Place five large spoonfuls of the mixture on to each baking sheet, spacing them well apart. Bake for 15 minutes until the cookies have risen. Leave on the baking sheet for 5 minutes to firm up, then transfer to a wire rack to cool.

Variation
To create pretty blossoming trees, attach pastel-coloured sugar flowers to the cookies instead of coloured sweets.

4 To decorate the cookies, mix together the icing sugar and lemon juice to make a thick paste. Use a little paste to secure one end of a chocolate finger to each cookie.

5 Attach the coloured sweets in the same way, securing each one with a little paste. Leave the cookies to set for at least 1 hour. (Handle the decorated cookies with care.)

Orange Biscotti

These crisp, crunchy cookies are based on a traditional Italian recipe in which the cookies are packed with nuts and baked twice. This version is flavoured with orange instead of the nuts and shaped into long, thin sticks. They are a little softer than the classic biscotti, which are very hard.

3 Bake the dough for 25 minutes, then remove from the oven and leave to stand for about 5 minutes until slightly cooled.

4 Using a sharp knife carefully cut the mixture widthways into thin sticks, about 1cm/½in wide.

5 Space the cookies out slightly on the baking sheet so there's a gap in between each one. (This will allow air to circulate between them.) Return them to the oven and bake for a further 20 minutes until crisp. Transfer the biscotti to a wire rack and leave to cool.

Makes about 20

50g/2oz/¼ cup unsalted (sweet) butter, at room temperature, diced
90g/3½oz/½ cup light muscovado (brown) sugar
1 egg
finely grated rind of 1 small orange, plus 10ml/2 tsp juice
175g/6oz/1½ cups self-raising (self-rising) flour
7.5ml/1½ tsp baking powder
good pinch of ground cinnamon
50g/2oz/½ cup polenta

1 Preheat the oven to 160°C/325°F/ Gas 3. Grease a large baking sheet. In a large bowl, beat together the butter and sugar until smooth and creamy. Beat in the egg, then the orange rind and juice, flour, baking powder, cinnamon and polenta.

2 Tip the mixture on to a lightly floured surface and knead. Place the dough on the baking sheet and flatten out with the palm of your hand to make a rectangle about 25 x 18cm/10 x 7in.

Ice-cream Sandwiches

Home-made wafer cookies have a flavour unlike anything you can buy at the supermarket. These crisp, nutty cookies make perfect ice-cream sandwiches for a summertime treat. They're also fun to make and are good accompaniments to almost any fruity or creamy dessert.

Makes 6 sandwiches
50g/2oz/¼ cup unsalted (sweet) butter
2 egg whites
75g/3oz/scant ½ cup caster
  (superfine) sugar
50g/2oz/½ cup plain (all-purpose) flour
40g/1½oz/scant ½ cup ground almonds
30ml/2 tbsp flaked (sliced) almonds
raspberry ripple or vanilla ice cream,
  to serve
icing (confectioners') sugar,
  for dusting

1 Preheat the oven to 200°C/400°F/ Gas 6. Line two large baking sheets with baking parchment. Put the butter in a small pan and melt over a very low heat.

2 Put the egg whites and sugar in a bowl and whisk lightly with a fork until the egg whites are just broken up. Add the flour, melted butter and ground almonds and mix until evenly combined.

3 Drop six level tablespoonfuls of mixture on to each baking sheet, spacing them well apart. Spread the mixture into 7cm/2¾in rounds.

4 Sprinkle with almonds and bake for 10 minutes, or until golden around the edges. Peel away the paper and cool on a wire rack.

5 Place a scoop of slightly softened ice cream on to one cookie and top with another, gently pressing them together. Dust with sugar and serve.

Cook's Tip
Don't be tempted to use greaseproof (waxed) paper instead of baking parchment as the cookies may stick to it.

Chunky Chocolate

Whether it's the merest smear on top of a plain cookie, a handful of chocolate chips placed in the cookie dough, or simply a full-on chocolate extravaganza, kids just love chocolate cookies. Try fun and frivolous ideas such as cookies on sticks or chocolate wands or go for a classic such as mini chocolate marylands or deliciously gooey chocolate thumbprint cookies.

Mini Chocolate Marylands

These tasty little cookies are perfect for any age group. They're easy to make and even children can get involved with helping to press the chocolate chips into the unbaked dough.

Makes 40–45
125g/4¼oz/generous ½ cup
*   unsalted (sweet) butter, at room*
*   temperature, diced*
90g/3½oz/ ½ cup caster
*   (superfine) sugar*
I egg
I egg yolk
5ml/I tsp vanilla essence (extract)
175g/6oz/I½ cups self-raising
*   (self-rising) flour*
90g/3½oz/generous ½ cup milk
90g/3½oz/generous ½ cup
*   chocolate chips*

I Preheat the oven to 180°C/350°F/ Gas 4. Grease two baking sheets.

2 In a large bowl, beat together the butter and sugar until pale and creamy. Add the egg, egg yolk, vanilla essence, flour, milk and half the chocolate chips and stir well until thoroughly combined.

3 Using 2 teaspoons, place small mounds of the mixture on the baking sheets, spacing them slightly apart to allow room for spreading.

4 Press the remaining chocolate chips on to the mounds of cookie dough and press down gently.

5 Bake for 10–15 minutes until pale golden. Leave the cookies on the baking sheet for 2 minutes to firm up, then transfer to a wire rack to cool completely.

Cook's Tip
This recipe makes quite a large quantity. If you like, you can freeze half of the cookies for another time. Simply thaw, then return to the oven for a few minutes to re-crisp before serving.

Fruity Chocolate Cookie-cakes

The combination of spongy cookie, fruity preserve and dark chocolate makes irresistible eating for kids of all ages. As cookies go, these are a little fiddly, but that's all part of the fun.

Makes 18
90g/3½oz/½ cup caster
*   (superfine) sugar*
2 eggs
50g/2oz/½ cup plain (all-purpose) flour
75g/3oz/6 tbsp apricot-orange
*   marmalade or apricot jam*
125g/4¼oz plain (semisweet) chocolate

1 Preheat the oven to 190°C/375°F/ Gas 5. Grease 18 patty tins (muffin pans), preferably non-stick. (If you don't have that many patty tins, you'll need to bake the cookies in batches.)

2 Stand a mixing bowl in very hot water for a couple of minutes to heat through, keeping the inside of the bowl dry. Put the sugar and eggs in the bowl and whisk with a hand-held electric mixer until light and frothy and the beaters leave a ribbon trail when lifted. Sift the flour over the mixture and stir in gently using a large metal spoon.

3 Divide the mixture among the patty tins. Bake for 10 minutes until just firm and pale golden around the edges. Using a palette knife (metal spatula), lift from the tins and transfer to a wire rack to cool.

4 Press the marmalade or jam through a sieve to remove any rind or fruit pieces. Spoon a little of the smooth jam on to the centre of each cookie.

5 Break the chocolate into pieces and place in a heatproof bowl set over a pan of gently simmering water. Heat, stirring frequently, until melted and smooth.

6 Spoon a little chocolate on to the top of each cookie and spread gently to the edges with a palette knife. Once the chocolate has just started to set, very gently press it with the back of a fork to give a textured surface. Leave to set for at least 1 hour.

Chocolate Wands

Shaping these long, wafery chocolate cookies is fun, but you need to work quickly so it might take a few attempts to get the technique just right. Only bake two cookies at a time; any more and they will become brittle before you have time to shape them into wands.

Makes 10–12
3 egg whites
90g/3½oz/½ cup caster (superfine) sugar
25g/1oz/2 tbsp unsalted (sweet)
   butter, melted
30ml/2 tbsp plain (all-purpose) flour
15ml/1 tbsp cocoa powder
   (unsweetened)
30ml/2 tbsp single (light) cream
90g/3½oz milk chocolate and
   multi-coloured sprinkles, to decorate

1 Preheat the oven to 180°C/350°F/ Gas 4. Line two large baking sheets with baking parchment and grease the paper well.

2 In a bowl, briefly beat together the egg whites and sugar until the whites are broken up.

3 Add the melted butter, flour, cocoa powder and cream to the egg whites and beat with a wooden spoon until smooth.

Cook's Tip
These cookies look best when the wands are really slender. Use a wooden spoon with a thin handle for shaping the cookies around. Alternatively, use a chunky pencil wrapped in kitchen foil.

4 Place 2 teaspoons of the mixture to one side of a baking sheet and spread the mixture into an oval shape, about 15cm/6in long. Spoon more mixture on to the other side of the baking sheet and shape in the same way.

5 Bake for 7–8 minutes until the edges begin to darken. Meanwhile, prepare two more cookies on the second baking sheet so you can put them in the oven while shaping the first batch into wands.

6 Leave the baked cookies on the paper for 30 seconds, then carefully lift one off and wrap it around the handle of a wooden spoon. As soon as it starts to hold its shape ease it off the spoon and shape the second cookie in the same way.

7 Continue baking and shaping the cookies in this way until all the mixture has been used up.

8 Break the chocolate into pieces and place in a heatproof bowl set over a pan of gently simmering water. Heat, stirring occasionally, until the chocolate has melted.

9 Dip the ends of the cookies in the chocolate, turning them until the ends are thickly coated.

10 Sprinkle the chocolate-coated ends of the cookies with coloured sprinkles and place on a sheet of baking parchment. Leave for about 1 hour until the chocolate has set.

Chocolate Caramel Nuggets

Inside each of these buttery cookies lies a soft-centred chocolate-coated caramel. They're at their most delicious served an hour or so after baking, so you might want to shape them in advance, then put the baking sheet of uncooked nuggets in the refrigerator until you are ready to bake them.

Makes 14

150g/5oz/1¼ cups self-raising
   (self-rising) flour
90g/3½oz/7 tbsp unsalted (sweet) butter,
   chilled and diced
50g/2oz/¼ cup golden caster
   (superfine) sugar
1 egg yolk
5ml/1 tsp vanilla essence (extract)
14 soft-centred chocolate caramels
icing (confectioners') sugar and cocoa
   powder (unsweetened), for dusting

1 Put the flour and diced butter in a food processor and process until the mixture resembles fairly fine breadcrumbs.

2 Add the sugar, egg yolk and vanilla essence to the food processor and process until a smooth dough forms. Wrap the dough in clear film (plastic wrap) and chill for 30 minutes.

3 Preheat the oven to 200°C/400°F/Gas 6. Grease a large baking sheet.

4 Roll out the dough thinly on a lightly floured surface and cut out 28 rounds using a 5cm/2in cutter.

5 Place one chocolate caramel on a cookie round, then lay a second round on top. Pinch the edges of the dough together so that the chocolate caramel is completely enclosed, then place on the baking sheet. Make the remaining cookies in the same way. Bake for about 10 minutes until pale golden.

6 Transfer to a wire rack and leave to cool. Serve lightly dusted with icing sugar and cocoa powder.

Chocolate Whirls

These cookies are so easy that you don't even have to make any dough. They're made with ready-made puff pastry rolled up with a chocolate filling. They're not too sweet and are similar to Danish pastries, so you could make them as a special treat for breakfast or brunch.

Makes about 20

75g/3oz/⅓ cup golden caster
   (superfine) sugar
40g/1½oz/6 tbsp cocoa powder
   (unsweetened)
2 eggs
500g/1lb 2oz puff pastry
25g/1oz/2 tbsp butter, softened
75g/3oz/generous ½ cup sultanas
   (golden raisins)
90g/3½oz milk chocolate

I Preheat the oven to 220°C/425°F/ Gas 7. Grease two baking sheets.

2 Put the sugar, cocoa powder and eggs in a bowl and mix to a paste.

3 Roll out the pastry on a lightly floured surface to make a 30cm/ 12in square. Trim off any rough edges using a sharp knife.

4 Dot the pastry all over with the softened butter, then spread with the chocolate paste and sprinkle the sultanas over the top.

Cook's Tip
Use a sharp knife to cut the cookie slices from the pastry roll, and wipe the blade clean with a cloth every few slices.

5 Roll the pastry into a sausage-shape, then cut the roll into 1cm/ ½in slices. Place the slices on the baking sheets, spacing them apart.

6 Bake the cookies for 10 minutes until risen and pale golden. Transfer to a wire rack and leave to cool.

7 Break the milk chocolate into pieces and put in a heatproof bowl set over a pan of gently simmering water. Heat, stirring frequently until melted and smooth.

8 Spoon or pipe lines of melted chocolate over the cookies, taking care not to completely hide the swirls of chocolate filling.

Chocolate Cookies on Sticks

Let your imagination run riot when decorating these fun chocolate cookies. Use plenty of brightly coloured sweets or create a real chocolate feast by only using chocolate decorations. Whichever you choose, these cookies are very sweet so should be kept as a real treat for special occasions.

3 Spoon the milk chocolate into the outlines on the paper, reserving one or two spoonfuls of chocolate. Using the back of a spoon, carefully spread the chocolate to the edges to make neat shapes.

4 Press the end of a wooden ice lolly stick into each of the shapes, and spoon over a little more melted milk chocolate to cover the stick. Sprinkle the chocolate shapes with the crumbled cookies.

5 Pipe or drizzle the cookies with the melted milk chocolate, then sprinkle the cookies with the coloured sweets, chocolate chips or chocolate-coated raisins, pressing them gently to make sure they stick.

6 Chill for about 1 hour until set, then carefully peel away the paper.

Makes 12

125g/4¼oz milk chocolate
75g/3oz white chocolate
50g/2oz chocolate-coated
* sweetmeal cookies, crumbled*
* into chunks*
a selection of small coloured sweets
* (candies), chocolate chips*
* or chocolate-coated raisins*
12 wooden ice lolly
* (popsicle) sticks*

1 Break the milk and white chocolate into pieces and put in separate heatproof bowls. Place each bowl in turn over a pan of gently simmering water and heat, stirring frequently, until melted.

2 Meanwhile, draw six 7cm/2¾in rounds on baking parchment and six 9 x 7cm/3½ x 2¾in rectangles. Invert the paper on to a large tray.

Chocolate Thumbprint Cookies

Chunky, chocolatey and gooey all at the same time, these gorgeous cookies are topped with a spoonful of chocolate spread after baking to really add to their indulgent feel. Use your favourite chocolate spread, whether it is plain, milk, white or nut-flavoured.

Makes 16

115g/4oz/½ cup unsalted (sweet) butter, at room temperature, diced
115g/4oz/generous ½ cup light muscovado (brown) sugar
1 egg
75g/3oz/⅔ cup plain (all-purpose) flour
25g/1oz/¼ cup cocoa powder (unsweetened)
2.5ml/½ tsp bicarbonate of soda (baking soda)
115g/4oz/generous 1 cup rolled oats
75–90ml/5–6 tbsp chocolate spread

1 Preheat the oven to 180°C/350°F/ Gas 4. Grease a large baking sheet. In a bowl, beat together the butter and sugar until creamy.

2 Add the egg, flour, cocoa powder, bicarbonate of soda and rolled oats to the bowl and mix well.

3 Using your hands, roll spoonfuls of the mixture into balls. Place the balls on the baking sheet, spacing them well apart to allow room for spreading. Flatten slightly.

4 Dip a thumb in flour and press into the centre of each cookie to make an indent. Bake the cookies for 10 minutes. Leave for 2 minutes, then transfer to a wire rack to cool.

5 Spoon a little chocolate spread into the indent on each cookie.

Chocolate Box Cookies

These prettily decorated, bitesize cookies look as though they've come straight out of a box of chocolates. They're great for a special tea or for wrapping as gifts, and older children will love getting thoroughly absorbed in making and decorating them.

Makes about 50

175g/6oz/1½ cups self-raising (self-rising) flour
25g/1oz/¼ cup cocoa powder (unsweetened)
5ml/1 tsp mixed spice (apple pie spice)
50g/2oz/¼ cup unsalted (sweet) butter, at room temperature, diced
115g/4oz/generous ½ cup caster (superfine) sugar
1 egg
1 egg yolk

FOR THE DECORATION

150g/5oz milk chocolate
150g/5oz white chocolate
100g/3¾oz plain (semisweet) chocolate
whole almonds or walnuts
cocoa powder, for dusting

1 Grease two baking sheets. Put the flour, cocoa powder, spice and butter into a food processor. Process until the ingredients are thoroughly blended. Add the sugar, egg and egg yolk to the processor and mix to a smooth dough.

2 Turn out the dough on to a lightly floured surface and knead gently. Cut the dough in half and roll out each piece under the palms of your hands to form two long logs, each 33cm/13in long.

3 Cut each log into 1cm/½in slices. Place the slices on the prepared baking sheets, spacing them slightly apart. Chill for at least 30 minutes. Meanwhile, preheat the oven to 180°C/350°F/ Gas 4.

4 Bake for 10 minutes until slightly risen. Transfer to a wire rack to cool.

5 To decorate, break the chocolate into three separate heatproof bowls. Place each bowl, in turn, over a pan of gently simmering water and stir frequently until melted.

6 Divide the cookies into six batches. Using a fork, dip one batch, a cookie at a time, into the milk chocolate to coat completely. Place on a sheet of baking parchment.

7 Taking the next batch of cookies, half-dip in milk chocolate and place on the baking parchment.

8 Continue with the next two batches of cookies and the white chocolate. Completely coat one batch, then half-coat the second.

9 Continue with the remaining cookies, completely coating one batch in the plain chocolate and half-dipping the other. Press a whole nut on to the tops of the plain chocolate-coated cookies.

10 Put the leftover white chocolate in a small plastic bag and squeeze it into one corner. Snip off the tip, then drizzle lines of chocolate over the milk chocolate-coated cookies.

11 Dust the white chocolate-coated cookies with a little cocoa powder. Store all the cookies in a cool place until ready to serve.

Cook's Tip
Once you have mastered the art of decorating the cookies, vary the combinations. Try drizzling milk or dark chocolate over the different cookies.

Chocolate Florentines

These big, flat, crunchy cookies are just like traditional florentines but use seeds instead of nuts. Rolling the edges in milk or white chocolate makes them feel like a real treat.

Makes 12

50g/2oz/¼ cup unsalted (sweet) butter
50g/2oz/¼ cup caster (superfine) sugar
15ml/1 tbsp milk
25g/1oz/scant ¼ cup pumpkin seeds
40g/1½oz/generous ¼ cup
  sunflower seeds
50g/2oz/scant ½ cup raisins
25g/1oz/2 tbsp multi-coloured glacé
  (candied) cherries, chopped
30ml/2 tbsp plain (all-purpose) flour
125g/4¼oz milk or white chocolate

1 Preheat the oven to 180°C/350°F/ Gas 4. Line two baking sheets with baking parchment and grease the paper well.

2 In a pan, melt the butter with the sugar, stirring, until the sugar has dissolved, then cook until bubbling. Remove the pan from the heat and stir in the milk, pumpkin and sunflower seeds, raisins, glacé cherries and flour. Mix well.

3 Spoon 6 teaspoonfuls of the mixture on to each baking sheet, spacing them well apart. Bake for 8–10 minutes until the cookies are turning dark golden. Using a palette knife (metal spatula), push back the edges of the cookies to neaten. Leave on the baking sheets for about 5 minutes to firm up, then transfer to a wire rack to cool.

4 Break up the chocolate and put in a heatproof bowl set over a pan of gently simmering water. Heat, stirring frequently, until melted. Roll the edges of the cookies in the chocolate and leave to set on a clean sheet of baking parchment for about 1 hour.

Variation
If you prefer, use plain (semisweet) chocolate to decorate the cookies.

Triple Chocolate Sandwiches

Chocolate shortbread makes a brilliant base for sandwiching and coating in lashings of delicious melted chocolate. Kids can enjoy making them as they don't need to be perfectly uniform.

Makes 15

125g/4¼oz/generous ½ cup unsalted
   (sweet) butter, chilled and diced
150g/5oz/1¼ cups plain
   (all-purpose) flour
30ml/2 tbsp cocoa powder (unsweetened)
50g/2oz/¼ cup caster (superfine) sugar
75g/3oz white chocolate
25g/1oz/2 tbsp unsalted (sweet) butter
115g/4oz milk chocolate

1 Put the butter, flour and cocoa in a food processor. Process until the mixture resembles breadcrumbs. Add the sugar and process again until the mixture forms a dough.

2 Transfer the dough to a clean surface and knead lightly. Wrap in clear film (plastic wrap) and chill for 30 minutes.

3 Preheat the oven to 200°C/400°F/Gas 6. Grease a large baking sheet.

4 Roll out the chilled dough on a floured surface to a 33 × 16cm/13 × 6¼in rectangle. Lift on to the baking sheet and trim the edges.

5 Cut the dough in half lengthways, then cut across at 2cm/¾in intervals to make 30 small bars.

6 Prick each bar with a fork and bake for 12–15 minutes until just beginning to darken around the edges. Remove from the oven and cut between the bars again while the cookies are still warm. Leave for 2 minutes, then transfer to a wire rack to cool.

7 To make the filling, break the white chocolate into a heatproof bowl. Add half the butter and set the bowl over a pan of gently simmering water and stir frequently until melted.

8 Spread a little of the filling evenly on to one of the bars. Place another bar on top and push together to sandwich the cookies. Continue in the same way with the remaining cookies and filling.

9 To make the topping, break the milk chocolate into a heatproof bowl. Add the remaining butter and set over a pan of simmering water and stir frequently until melted. Using a teaspoon, drizzle the chocolate over the top of the cookies, then leave to set.

Time to Party

There's nothing quite like an extra-special cookie to make a kids' party go with a swing. This chapter is packed with fun ideas that kids will love, including cookie bracelets to slip around the wrist, novelty cookies that look like mini pizzas or a giant birthday cookie studded with candles to take the place of the more traditional birthday cake.

Stained Glass Windows

Baking coloured sweets inside a cookie frame creates a stunning stained glass effect, particularly if you hang the cookies in front of a window or near a lamp or wall light where the light can shine through. The translucent cookie centre will stay brittle for a day or so before softening and finally melting, so don't be tempted to hang them up for too long.

Makes 12–14

175g/6oz/1½ cups plain
  (all-purpose) flour
2.5ml/½ tsp bicarbonate of soda
  (baking soda)
2.5ml/½ tsp ground cinnamon
75g/3oz/6 tbsp unsalted (sweet)
  butter, chilled and diced
75g/3oz/scant ½ cup caster
  (superfine) sugar
30ml/2 tbsp golden (light
  corn) syrup
1 egg yolk
150g/5oz brightly coloured, clear
  boiled sweets (hard candies)

1 Put the flour, bicarbonate of soda, cinnamon and butter into a food processor. Process until the mixture resembles breadcrumbs.

2 Add the sugar, syrup and egg yolk to the food processor, then process again until the mixture starts to cling together in a dough.

3 Turn the dough out on to a lightly floured surface and knead until smooth. Wrap in clear film (plastic wrap) and chill in the refrigerator for at least 30 minutes.

4 Preheat the oven to 180°C/350°F/Gas 4. Line two large baking sheets with baking parchment.

5 Roll out the dough thinly on a lightly floured surface. Cut into 6cm/2½in wide strips, then cut diagonally across the strips to create about 12 diamond shapes.

6 Carefully transfer the diamond shapes to the lined baking sheets, spacing them slightly apart.

7 Using a sharp knife, cut out a smaller diamond shape from the centre of each cookie and remove to leave a 1cm/½in frame.

8 Using a skewer, make a hole at one end of each cookie (large enough to thread fine ribbon).

9 Bake the the cookies for about 5 minutes. Meanwhile, lightly crush the sweets (still in their wrappers) by tapping them gently with the end of a rolling pin.

10 Remove the cookies from the oven and quickly fill the centre of each one with about two crushed sweets of the same colour.

11 Return the cookies to the oven for a further 5 minutes until the sweets have melted. Remove from the oven and use a skewer to re-mark the skewer holes if they have shrunk during baking.

12 If the sweets haven't spread to fill the cookie centre during baking, while still hot, carefully spread the melted sweets with the tip of a skewer.

13 Leave the cookies on the baking parchment until the melted sweets have hardened. Once the centres are hard, gently peel away the paper from the cookies.

14 Thread fine ribbon of different lengths through the holes in the cookies, then hang as decorations around the home.

Cook's Tip
Make sure you re-mark the skewer holes while the cookies are still hot as they'll probably break if you try to make the holes once they've cooled.

Gold Medals

These cookies are really good for kids' parties. You can present each child with a huge cookie medal when they sit down at the table, or hand them out to winners of party games. Alternatively, they make great going-home gifts when children leave.

Makes 10

50g/2oz/¼ cup unsalted (sweet) butter,
  at room temperature, diced
115g/4oz/generous ½ cup caster
  (superfine) sugar
1 egg
150g/5oz/1¼ cups self-raising
  (self-rising) flour
1.5ml/¼ tsp bicarbonate of soda
  (baking soda)

FOR THE DECORATION

1 egg white
200g/7oz/1¾ cups icing
  (confectioners') sugar
small brightly coloured sweets (candies)

1 Preheat the oven to 180°C/350°F/ Gas 4. Grease two baking sheets with a little butter.

2 In a bowl, beat together the butter and sugar until smooth and creamy, then beat in the egg. Add the flour and bicarbonate of soda and mix well to combine.

3 Place large spoonfuls of the mixture on the baking sheets, spacing them well apart to allow room for spreading. Bake for about 15 minutes, or until pale golden and slightly risen.

4 Using a skewer, make quite a large hole in the cookie, 1cm/½in from the edge. Transfer to a wire rack and leave to cool.

5 To make the icing, beat the egg white in a bowl using a wooden spoon. Gradually beat in the icing sugar to make a thick paste that just holds its shape. Spoon the icing into a small plastic bag and snip off the merest tip.

6 Write icing numbers or messages in the centre of the cookies. Secure a circle of sweets around the edge of each cookie with a little of the icing, then leave to set.

7 Once the icing has hardened, carefully thread each cookie with a piece of ribbon.

Party Bracelets

These tiny cookies are threaded on to fine elastic or ribbon along with an assortment of brightly coloured sweets that have a ready-made hole in the middle. Make the cookies a day or two in advance and simply thread together with the sweets on the day of the party.

Makes 10

*50g/2oz/¼ cup unsalted (sweet) butter,
    at room temperature, diced*
*115g/4oz/generous ½ cup caster
    (superfine) sugar*
5ml/1 tsp vanilla essence (extract)
pink or green food colouring
1 egg
*200g/7oz/1¾ cups self-raising
    (self-rising) flour*

FOR THE DECORATION
*2 large bags of boiled sweets (hard
    candies) with holes in the centre*
*narrow pastel-coloured ribbon,
    for threading*

1 In a bowl, beat together the butter, sugar and vanilla essence until pale and creamy. Add a dash of pink or green food colouring, then beat in the egg. Add the flour and mix well to form a dough. Grease two baking sheets.

2 Turn out the dough on to a lightly floured surface and roll out under the palms of your hands into two long, thin sausage shapes, each about 40cm/16in long. Cut each roll across using a large sharp knife into 5mm/¼in lengths.

3 Space the rounds of dough slightly apart on the baking sheets. Place the baking sheets in the refrigerator for about 30 minutes. Preheat the oven to 180°C/350°F/ Gas 4.

4 Bake the cookies for about 8 minutes until slightly risen and beginning to colour. Remove from the oven and, using a skewer, immediately make holes for the ribbon to be threaded through. (You may find it easier to bake one sheet of cookies at a time.) Transfer the cookies to a wire rack to cool.

5 Thread the cookies on to 55cm/ 22in lengths of narrow elastic or ribbon, alternating with the sweets. (You should end up with about seven cookies on each ribbon.) Tie the ends of the elastic or ribbons together in bows to finish.

Cook's Tip
When you make the holes in the cookies, you will need to work quickly. If the cookies start to harden before you have time to make holes in all of them, pop the remaining cookies back in the oven very briefly to re-soften.

Name Cookies

You could decorate these cookies for each of the children coming to a party, either in vibrant, bright colours or in more delicate pastels. Prop a name cookie up against the glass at each place setting around the tea table and let the children find their own seats.

Makes 20

200g/7oz/scant 1 cup unsalted (sweet) butter, chilled and diced
300g/10oz/2½ cups plain (all-purpose) flour
finely grated rind of 1 orange
90g/3½oz/scant 1 cup icing (confectioners') sugar
2 egg yolks

FOR THE DECORATION

1 egg white
200g/7oz/1¾ cups icing sugar
2 different food colourings
jelly beans or silver balls

1 Put the butter, flour and orange rind in a food processor and process until the mixture resembles fine breadcrumbs. Add the icing sugar and egg yolks and blend until smooth. Wrap in clear film (plastic wrap) and chill for 30 minutes.

2 Preheat the oven to 200°C/400°F/ Gas 6. Grease two baking sheets.

3 Roll out the dough on a floured surface and cut out cookies in a variety of shapes, such as squares, hearts and rounds. Make sure each cookie is at least 7.5cm/3in across.

4 Transfer the cookies to the baking sheets, spacing them slightly apart and bake for 10–12 minutes until pale golden around the edges.

5 Leave the cookies on the baking sheet for about 2 minutes to firm up, then transfer to a wire rack to cool completely.

6 To make the icing, put the egg white and icing sugar in a bowl and beat together until smooth, and the icing only just holds its shape.

7 Divide the icing between two bowls, then beat a few drops of food colouring into each bowl, to make two different colours.

8 Spoon the two different icings into separate small plastic bags and gently squeeze into one corner.

Variation
If you prefer, add food colouring to only one of the bowls of icing, leaving the second bowl of icing white. This can look very pretty, particularly if you choose a pastel colour for the second bowl of icing and decorate with silver balls.

9 Cut off the merest tip from each bag so the icing can be piped in a very thin line, then write the names or initials of party guests on the cookies. Pipe decorative borders around the edges of the cookies using both colours of icing. Use either straight lines, flutes, dots of icing or squiggled lines of piping to decorate.

10 Chop the jelly beans, if using, into small pieces. Secure the jelly beans or the silver balls on to the icing on the cookies to finish. Leave the cookies to set for at least 1 hour.

Giant Birthday Cookie

This enormous cookie is one for cookie-lovers of any age. Complete with candles, it makes the perfect party centrepiece. To personalize the cookie, write the recipient's name on top in icing.

Makes one 28cm/11in cookie
175g/6oz/¾ cup unsalted
(sweet) butter, at room
temperature, diced
125g/4¼oz/⅓ cup light muscovado
(brown) sugar
1 egg yolk
175g/6oz/1½ cups plain
(all-purpose) flour
5ml/1 tsp bicarbonate of soda
(baking soda)
finely grated rind of 1 orange
or lemon
75g/3oz/scant 1 cup rolled oats

FOR THE DECORATION
125g/4¼oz/generous ½ cup
cream cheese
225g/8oz/2 cups icing
(confectioners') sugar
5–10ml/1–2 tsp lemon juice
birthday candles
white and milk chocolate-coated
raisins or peanuts
cocoa powder, for dusting
gold or silver balls, for sprinkling

1 Preheat the oven to 190°C/375°F/ Gas 5. Grease a 28cm/11in loose-based flan tin (tart pan) and place on a large baking sheet.

2 Put the butter and the sugar in a large bowl and beat together until pale and creamy.

3 Add the egg yolk to the butter and sugar mixture and stir well to mix. Add the flour, bicarbonate of soda, grated orange or lemon rind and rolled oats and stir thoroughly until evenly combined.

4 Turn the mixture into the tin and flatten with a wet wooden spoon.

5 Bake for 15–20 minutes until risen and golden. Leave to cool in the tin. (If any of the mixture has seeped under the ring during baking trim it off with a knife while still warm.)

6 Carefully slide the cookie from the tin on to a large, flat serving plate or board.

7 Make the frosting. Beat the cream cheese in a bowl, then add the icing sugar and 5ml/1 tsp of the lemon juice. Beat until smooth and peaking, adding more juice if required.

8 Spoon the mixture into a piping (pastry) bag and pipe swirls around the edge of the cookie. Press the candles into the frosting. Sprinkle with chocolate raisins or peanuts and dust with cocoa powder. Finish by sprinkling with gold or silver balls.

Mini Party Pizzas

These cute little cookie confections look amazingly realistic and older children will love them. They're simple and fun to make, with a basic cookie topped with icing, marzipan and dark cherries.

Makes 16

90g/3½oz/7 tbsp unsalted (sweet) butter, at room temperature, diced
90g/3½oz/½ cup golden caster (superfine) sugar
15ml/1 tbsp golden (light corn) syrup
175g/6oz/1½ cups self-raising (self-rising) flour

FOR THE TOPPING

150g/5oz/1¼ cups icing (confectioners') sugar
20–25ml/4–5 tsp lemon juice
red food colouring
90g/3½oz yellow marzipan, grated
8 dark glacé (candied) cherries, halved
a small piece of angelica, finely chopped

1 Preheat the oven to 180°C/350°F/ Gas 4. Grease two baking sheets.

2 In a bowl, beat together the butter and sugar until creamy. Beat in the syrup, then add the flour and mix to a smooth paste.

3 Turn the mixture on to a lightly floured surface and cut into 16 even-size pieces. Roll each piece into a ball between the palms of your hands, then space well apart on the baking sheets, slightly flattening each one.

4 Bake for about 12 minutes, or until pale golden. Leave on the baking sheets for 3 minutes, then transfer to a wire rack to cool.

5 To make the topping, put the icing sugar in a bowl and stir in enough lemon juice to make a fairly thick, spreadable paste. Beat in enough food colouring to make the paste a deep red colour.

Cook's Tip
Make sure you use a red food colouring rather than cochineal, which will colour the icing pink. Red food colouring is more readily available in paste form.

6 Spread the icing to within 5mm/ ¼in of the edges of the cookies. Sprinkle with the grated marzipan and place a halved cherry in the centre. Arrange a few pieces of chopped angelica on top so that the cookies resemble little cheese and tomato pizzas.

Silly Faces

These funny little characters can be made using almost any type of cookie mix, as long as the baked cookies are quite big and not too craggy. Silly faces are great fun for kids to decorate as they can really go to town, experimenting with different hairstyles and features.

5 Bake for 10–12 minutes until turning golden around the edges. Transfer to a wire rack to cool.

6 To make the icing, beat together the butter and icing sugar in a bowl until smooth and creamy.

7 Using a small palette knife (metal spatula) spread a little buttercream along the top edge of each cookie, then secure the strawberry, apple or liquorice strands. Either snip the strands to make straight hair, or twist the strands to make curly hair.

8 Use a dot of buttercream to secure a glacé cherry to the middle of each cookie for a nose. Pipe eyes and mouths using the writer icing, then add halved sweets, attached with buttercream, for the centres of the eyes.

Makes 14

115g/4oz/½ cup unsalted (sweet) butter, at room temperature, diced
115g/4oz/generous ½ cup golden caster (superfine) sugar
1 egg
115g/4oz/scant ⅓ cup golden (light corn) syrup
400g/14oz/3½ cups self-raising (self-rising) flour

FOR THE DECORATION

75g/3oz/6 tbsp unsalted (sweet) butter, at room temperature, diced
150g/5oz/1¼ cups icing (confectioners') sugar
strawberry, apple or liquorice strands
glacé (candied) cherries, halved
red and black writer icing
small multi-coloured sweets (candies)

1 Put the butter and sugar in a large bowl and beat together until pale and creamy. Beat in the egg and golden syrup, then add the flour and mix together to make a thick paste.

2 Turn the mixture on to a lightly floured surface and knead until smooth. Wrap in clear film (plastic wrap) and chill for 30 minutes.

3 Preheat the oven to 180°C/350°F/ Gas 4. Grease two baking sheets.

4 Roll out the chilled dough on a lightly floured surface and cut out rounds using a 9cm/3½in round cookie cutter. Transfer the rounds to the baking sheets, re-rolling the trimmings to make more cookies.

Gingerbread House Cookies

For a party of young children, these gingerbread house cookies provide plenty of entertainment. You could incorporate a house decorating session as one of the party games, allowing the children to design their own house and take it home after the party.

Makes 10

115g/4oz/½ cup unsalted (sweet)
    butter, at room temperature, diced
115g/4oz/generous ½ cup light
    muscovado (brown) sugar
1 egg
115g/4oz/scant ⅓ cup black treacle
    (molasses) or golden (light corn) syrup
400g/14oz/3½ cups self-raising
    (self-rising) flour
5ml/1 tsp ground ginger (optional)

FOR THE DECORATION

1 tube white decorating icing
1 tube pastel-coloured decorating icing
selection of small multi-coloured sweets
    (candies), sugar flowers and silver balls

1 Put the butter and sugar in a large bowl and beat together until pale and creamy. Beat in the egg and treacle or syrup, then add the flour and ginger, if using. Mix together to make a thick paste.

2 Turn the mixture on to a lightly floured surface and knead until smooth. Wrap in clear film (plastic wrap) and chill for 30 minutes.

3 Preheat the oven to 180°C/350°F/ Gas 4. Grease three baking sheets. On a piece of paper, draw an 11 x 8cm/4¼ x 3¼in rectangle. Add a pitched roof and draw on a door and windows. Cut out the shapes to use as a template.

4 Roll out the dough on a floured surface. (It might be easier to roll out half the dough at a time.)

5 Using the template, cut out house shapes. Transfer to the baking sheets and re-roll the trimmings to make more. Bake for 12–15 minutes until risen and golden. Transfer the cookies to a wire rack to cool.

6 Use the icing in the tubes to pipe roof tiles, window and door frames and other decorative touches. Secure sweets and decorations to finish, cutting them into smaller pieces if preferred.

Jelly Bean Cones

Chocolate-dipped cookie cones filled with jelly beans are surprisingly easy to make. The filled cones look very pretty arranged in glasses or other small containers to keep them upright. This way they can double as a special treat and a delightful table decoration.

Makes 10

3 egg whites

90g/3½oz/½ cup caster (superfine) sugar

25g/1oz/2 tbsp unsalted (sweet) butter, melted

40g/1½oz/⅓ cup plain (all-purpose) flour

30ml/2 tbsp single (light) cream

90g/3½oz plain (semisweet) chocolate

jelly beans or other small sweets (candies)

1 Preheat the oven to 190°C/375°F/ Gas 5. Line two baking sheets with baking parchment and grease lightly.

2 Put the egg whites and sugar in a bowl and whisk lightly with a fork until the egg whites are broken up. Add the melted butter, flour and cream and stir well to make a smooth batter.

3 Using a 15ml/1 tbsp measure, place a rounded tablespoon of the mixture on one side of a baking sheet. Spread to a 9cm/3½in round with the back of the spoon. Spoon more mixture on to the other side of the baking sheet and spread out to make another round.

4 Bake for about 8–10 minutes until the edges are deep golden. Meanwhile, spoon two more rounds of cookie mixture on to the second baking sheet.

5 Remove the first batch of cookies from the oven and replace with the second batch. Peel away the paper from the baked cookies and roll them into cone shapes. Leave to set. Continue in this way until you have made ten cones.

6 Break the chocolate into a heatproof bowl set over a pan of simmering water and stir until melted. Dip the wide ends of the cookies in the chocolate and prop them inside narrow glasses to set, then fill with jelly beans or sweets.

Fortune Cookies

Chinese fortune cookies are light and wafery, and what they lack in substance, they certainly make up for in their fun capacity. These are great for older kids, who can prepare birthday messages, jokes or predictions to tuck into the cookies as soon as they're baked.

Makes 18

3 egg whites
50g/2oz/ ½ cup icing
  (confectioners') sugar
40g/1½oz/3 tbsp unsalted (sweet)
  butter, melted
50g/2oz/ ½ cup plain (all-purpose) flour

1 Preheat the oven to 200°C/400°F/ Gas 6. Line two baking sheets with baking parchment and grease. Cut a piece of paper into 18 small strips, measuring 6 × 2cm/2½ × ¾in. Write a message on each one.

2 Lightly whisk the egg whites and icing sugar until the whites are broken up. Add the butter and flour and beat until smooth.

3 Using a 10ml/2 tsp measure, spoon a little of the paste on to the baking sheet and spread to a 7.5cm/3in round with the back of a spoon. Add two more spoonfuls of mixture to the baking sheet and shape in the same way.

4 Bake for about 6 minutes until the cookies are golden. Meanwhile, prepare three more cookies on the second baking sheet.

5 Remove the first batch of cookies from the oven and replace with the second batch.

6 Working quickly, peel a hot cookie from the paper and fold it in half, tucking a message inside the fold. Rest the cookie over the rim of a glass or bowl and, very gently, fold again. (It probably won't fold over completely.) Fold the remaining two cookies in the same way.

7 Continue to bake and shape the remaining cookies in the same way until all the batter and messages have been used.

Cook's Tips
• *The secret to success is to spread the batter as thinly as possible on the paper. This will give a really crisp, light result.*
• *Don't be tempted to bake more than three cookies at once or they'll harden before you can shape them.*

Bars and Squares

From sticky chocolate brownies to oaty flapjacks packed with dried fruit and nuts, kids always seem to love traybakes. They're so easy to make and don't require the time-consuming rolling, cutting and shaping of some other types of cookie. Simply press the mixture into a baking tray or tin, pop in the oven and, once baked, cut into squares, wedges or bars.

White Chocolate Brownies

These irresistible brownies are packed full of creamy white chocolate and juicy sultanas. They are best served cut into very small portions as they are incredibly rich – but also because kids seem to find something utterly irresistible about the tiny, bitesize cookies.

Makes 18

75g/3oz/6 tbsp unsalted (sweet)
  butter, diced
400g/14oz white chocolate, chopped
3 eggs
90g/3½oz/½ cup golden caster
  (superfine) sugar
10ml/2 tsp vanilla essence (extract)
90g/3½oz/¾ cup sultanas
  (golden raisins)
coarsely grated rind of 1 lemon, plus
  15ml/1 tbsp juice
200g/7oz/1¾ cups plain
  (all-purpose) flour

1 Preheat the oven to 190°C/375°F/ Gas 5. Grease and line a 28 x 20cm/ 11 x 8in shallow baking tin (pan) with baking parchment.

2 Put the butter and 300g/11oz of the chocolate in a bowl and melt over a pan of gently simmering water, stirring frequently.

3 Remove the bowl from the heat and beat in the eggs and sugar, then add the vanilla essence, sultanas, lemon rind and juice, flour and the remaining chocolate.

4 Tip the mixture into the tin and spread into the corners. Bake for about 20 minutes until slightly risen and the surface is only just turning golden. The centre should still be slightly soft. Leave to cool in the tin.

5 Cut the brownies into small squares and remove from the tin.

Fudge-nut Bars

Although your kids will be desperate to tuck into these fudgy treats, it's well worth chilling them for a few hours before slicing so that they can be cut into neat pieces. You can use any kind of nut from mild-flavoured almonds, peanuts or macadamia nuts to slightly stronger pecans or hazelnuts.

Makes 16

150g/5oz/10 tbsp unsalted (sweet) butter,
   chilled and diced
250g/9oz/2¼ cups plain
   (all-purpose) flour
75g/3oz/scant ½ cup caster
   (superfine) sugar

FOR THE TOPPING

150g/5oz milk chocolate, broken
   into pieces
40g/1½oz/3 tbsp unsalted butter
400g/14oz can sweetened
   condensed milk
50g/2oz/½ cup chopped nuts

1 Preheat the oven to 160°C/325°F/ Gas 3. Grease a 28 × 18cm/11 × 7in shallow baking tin (pan).

2 Put the butter and flour in a food processor and process until the mixture resembles breadcrumbs. Add the sugar and blend again until the mixture starts to cling together.

3 Tip the mixture into the baking tin and spread out with the back of a wooden spoon to fill the base in an even layer. Bake for 35–40 minutes until the surface is very lightly coloured.

4 To make the topping, put the chocolate in a heavy pan with the butter and condensed milk. Heat gently until the chocolate and butter have melted, then increase the heat and cook, stirring, for 3–5 minutes until the mixture starts to thicken.

5 Add the chopped nuts to the pan and pour the mixture over the cookie base, spreading it in an even layer. Leave to cool, then chill for at least 2 hours until firm. Serve cut into bars.

Sticky Treacle Slices

This three-layered treat of buttery cookie base covered with a sticky dried fruit filling followed by an oaty flapjack-style topping is utterly delicious and unbelievably easy to make.

Makes 14

175g/6oz/1½ cups plain
  (all-purpose) flour
90g/3½oz/7 tbsp unsalted (sweet)
  butter, diced
50g/2oz/¼ cup caster (superfine) sugar
250g/9oz/generous 1 cup mixed dried
  fruit, such as prunes, apricots, peaches,
  pears and apples
300ml/½ pint/1¼ cups apple or
  orange juice
225g/8oz/⅔ cup golden (light
  corn) syrup
finely grated rind of 1 small orange,
  plus 45ml/3 tbsp juice
90g/3½oz/1 cup rolled oats

1 Preheat the oven to 180°C/350°F/ Gas 4. Grease a 28 x 18cm/11 x 7in shallow baking tin (pan).

2 Put the flour and butter in a food processor and process until the mixture begins to resemble fine breadcrumbs. Add the sugar and mix until the dough starts to cling together in a ball.

3 Tip the mixture into the baking tin and press down in an even layer with the back of a fork. Bake for about 15 minutes until the surface is just beginning to colour.

4 Meanwhile, prepare the filling. Remove the stones (pits) from any of the dried fruits, if not already done. Chop the fruit fairly finely and put in a pan with the fruit juice. Bring to the boil, reduce the heat and cover with a lid. Simmer gently for about 15 minutes, or until all the juice has been absorbed.

5 Leaving the base in the tin, tip the dried fruit filling on top and spread out in an even layer with the back of a spoon.

6 Put the golden syrup in a bowl with the orange rind and juice and oats and mix together. Spoon the mixture over the fruits, spreading it out evenly. Return to the oven for 25 minutes. Leave to cool in the tin for several hours before cutting into squares or bars.

Jewelled Shortbread Fingers

These shortbread fingers are made using a classic, buttery shortbread base, drizzled with icing and decorated with sparkling, crushed sweets and glistening gold or silver balls.

Makes 14

90g/3½oz/7 tbsp unsalted (sweet)
   butter, diced
175g/6oz/1½ cups plain
   (all-purpose) flour
50g/2oz/¼ cup caster (superfine) sugar

TO DECORATE

150g/5oz/1¼ cups icing
   (confectioners') sugar
10–15ml/2–3 tsp lemon juice
coloured boiled sweets (hard candies)
gold or silver balls

1 Preheat the oven to 160°C/325°F/ Gas 3. Grease an 18cm/7in square shallow baking tin (pan).

2 Put the butter and flour in a food processor and process until the mixture resembles breadcrumbs. Add the sugar and process until the ingredients cling together.

3 Put the dough in the baking tin and press down in an even layer using the back of a spoon. Bake for 35 minutes, or until just beginning to colour. Leave to cool in the tin.

4 To make the topping, put the icing sugar in a bowl and add enough lemon juice to make a thick paste that only just holds its shape.

5 Tap the boiled sweets (in their wrappers) gently with a rolling pin to break them into small pieces. Unwrap the sweets and mix them together in a bowl.

Cook's Tip

Use a serrated knife and a sawing action to cut the shortbread into neat fingers.

6 Turn out the shortbread base on to a board. Cut in half, then across into fingers. Drizzle with the icing, then sprinkle with the sweets and gold or silver balls. Leave to set.

Rainbow Gingerbread Squares

These gingerbread squares have a more spongy texture than traditional gingerbread cookies and look stunning decorated with vibrantly coloured sprinkles. Ground and preserved stem ginger gives a really spicy flavour, but can easily be left out for younger children.

Makes 16

225g/8oz/2 cups plain
   (all-purpose) flour
5ml/1 tsp baking powder
10ml/2 tsp ground ginger
2 pieces preserved stem ginger from
   a jar, finely chopped
90g/3½oz/¾ cup raisins
50g/2oz/¼ cup glacé (candied)
   cherries, chopped
115g/4oz/½ cup unsalted (sweet)
   butter, diced
115g/4oz/⅓ cup golden (light
   corn) syrup
30ml/2 tbsp black treacle (molasses)
75g/3oz/⅓ cup dark muscovado
   (molasses) sugar
2 eggs, beaten

FOR THE DECORATION

200g/7oz/1¾ cups icing
   (confectioners') sugar
50g/2oz/¼ cup unsalted (sweet) butter,
   at room temperature, diced
multi-coloured sprinkles

1 Preheat the oven to 160°C/325°F/ Gas 3. Grease a 20cm/8in square shallow baking or cake tin (pan) and line with baking parchment.

2 Sift the flour, baking powder and ground ginger into a bowl. Add the stem ginger, raisins and cherries and stir together well.

3 Put the butter, syrup, treacle and muscovado sugar in a small pan and heat gently until the butter melts. Pour the mixture into the dry ingredients. Add the eggs and stir well until evenly combined.

4 Tip the mixture into the baking tin and spread in an even layer, using the back of a wooden spoon. Bake for about 55 minutes, or until risen and firm in the centre. Leave to cool in the tin.

5 To make the topping, put the icing sugar and butter in a bowl with 20ml/4 tsp hot water and beat together until smooth and creamy.

6 Turn the gingerbread out of the baking tin on to a board. Using a large, sharp knife, carefully cut the gingerbread into 16 squares.

7 Using a teaspoon, drizzle a thick line of icing around the top edge of each gingerbread square. Don't worry if it falls down the sides. (If the icing is too stiff and doesn't come off the spoon easily, stir a little more hot water into the icing, about 5ml/1 tsp.)

8 Scatter the coloured sprinkles over the icing to finish and leave to set before serving.

Marshmallow Toasties

These soft cookie squares topped with a layer of strawberry jam and melted marshmallow make a sweet, sticky treat for kids of all ages. When you're toasting the marshmallows, watch them very closely because once they start to colour, they brown extremely quickly.

Makes 12

130g/4½oz/generous ½ cup unsalted (sweet) butter, at room temperature, diced
75g/3oz/scant ½ cup caster (superfine) sugar
finely grated rind of 1 lemon
10ml/2 tsp vanilla essence (extract)
75g/3oz/¾ cup ground almonds
1 egg
115g/4oz/1 cup self-raising (self-rising) flour
150g/5oz/½ cup strawberry jam
200g/7oz pink and white marshmallows
icing (confectioners') sugar, for dusting

1 Preheat the oven to 180°C/350°F/ Gas 4. Grease the base and sides of a 23cm/9in square baking tin (pan) and line with baking parchment.

2 Put the butter, sugar and lemon rind in a bowl and beat togethr until creamy. Beat in the vanilla essence, ground almonds and egg, then add the flour and stir well.

3 Turn the mixture into the tin and spread in an even layer. Bake for 20 minutes until pale golden and just firm. Leave to cool in the tin for 10 minutes.

4 Spread the cookie base with jam. Cut the marshmallows in half using scissors. Arrange, cut side down, in an even layer over the jam. Preheat the grill (broiler) to medium.

5 Put the tin under the grill for about 2 minutes until the marshmallows are melted and pale golden. Remove from the heat and gently press down each marshmallow with the back of a spoon to create an even layer of melted marshmallow. Return to the grill for a further minute until the surface is very toasted. Leave to cool.

6 To serve, dust lightly with icing sugar and cut into 12 squares or bars and remove from the tin.

Fruity Lemon Drizzle Bars

These tangy iced, spongy bars are great for popping in lunch boxes or for kids to snack on after school. The mixture of lemon and sultanas is lovely but you can easily experiment with other combinations such as orange and dried apricots or lime and dried pineapples.

Makes 16

250g/9oz ready-made sweet
  shortcrust pastry
90g/3¼oz/¾ cup self-raising
  (self-rising) flour
75g/3oz/¾ cup fine or
  medium oatmeal
5ml/1 tsp baking powder
130g/4½oz/generous ½ cup light
  muscovado (brown) sugar
2 eggs
150g/5oz/10 tbsp unsalted
  (sweet) butter, at room
  temperature, diced
finely grated rind of 1 lemon
90g/3½oz/¾ cup sultanas
  (golden raisins)
150g/5oz/1¼ cups icing
  (confectioners') sugar
15–30ml/3–4 tsp lemon juice

1 Preheat the oven to 190°C/375°F/Gas 5 and place a baking sheet in the oven to heat through. Generously grease a 28 × 18cm/11 × 7in shallow baking tin (pan).

2 Roll out the pastry thinly on a lightly floured, clean surface. Use to line the base of the baking tin, pressing the pastry up the sides. (Don't worry about rough edges.)

3 Put the flour, oatmeal, baking powder, sugar, eggs, butter and lemon rind in a mixing bowl. Beat with a hand-held electric whisk for about 2 minutes until pale and creamy. Stir in the sultanas.

4 Tip the filling into the pastry case and spread evenly into the corners using the back of a spoon.

5 Place the tin on the heated baking sheet in the oven and bake for about 30 minutes until pale golden and the surface feels firm to the touch.

6 Put the icing sugar in a small bowl with enough lemon juice to mix to a thin paste, about the consistency of pouring (half-and-half) cream.

7 Using a teaspoon, drizzle the icing diagonally across the warm cake in thin lines. Leave to cool in the tin.

8 When the icing has set, use a sharp knife to cut the cake in half lengthways. Cut each half across into 8 even-size bars.

Fruity Breakfast Bars

Instead of buying fruit and cereal bars from the supermarket, try making this quick and easy version – they are much tastier and more nutritious than most of the commercially made ones. They can be stored in an airtight container for up to four days.

Makes 12

270g/10oz jar apple sauce
115g/4oz/½ cup ready-to-eat dried
    apricots, chopped
115g/4oz/¾ cup raisins
50g/2oz/¼ cup demerara (raw) sugar
50g/2oz/⅓ cup sunflower seeds
25g/1oz/2 tbsp sesame seeds
25g/1oz/¼ cup pumpkin seeds
75g/3oz/scant 1 cup rolled oats
75g/3oz/⅔ cup self-raising (self-rising)
    wholemeal (whole-wheat) flour
50g/2oz/⅔ cup desiccated (dry
    unsweetened shredded) coconut
2 eggs

Cook's Tip

Allow the baking parchment to hang over the edges of the tin; this makes baked bars easier to remove.

1 Preheat the oven to 200°C/400°F/ Gas 6. Grease a 20cm/8in square shallow baking tin (pan) and line with baking parchment.

2 Put the apple sauce in a large bowl with the apricots, raisins, sugar and the sunflower, sesame and pumpkin seeds and stir together with a wooden spoon until thoroughly mixed.

3 Add the oats, flour, coconut and eggs to the fruit mixture and gently stir together until evenly combined.

4 Turn the mixture into the tin and spread to the edges in an even layer. Bake for about 25 minutes or until golden and just firm to the touch.

5 Leave to cool in the tin, then lift out on to a board and cut into bars.

Chewy Flapjacks

Flapjacks are about the easiest cookies to make and, with a little guidance, can be knocked up in minutes by even the youngest cooks. This chunky, chewy version is flavoured with orange rind, but you can substitute with other fruits such as a handful of raisins, chopped prunes or apricots.

Makes 18

250g/9oz/generous 1 cup unsalted
   (sweet) butter
finely grated rind of 1 large orange
225g/8oz/⅔ cup golden (light corn) syrup
75g/3oz/⅓ cup light muscovado
   (brown) sugar
375g/13oz/3¾ cups rolled oats

1 Preheat the oven to 180°C/350°F/Gas 4. Line the base and sides of a 28 x 20cm/11 x 8in shallow baking tin (pan) with baking parchment.

2 Put the butter, orange rind, syrup and sugar in a large pan and heat gently until the butter has melted.

3 Add the oats to the pan and stir to mix thoroughly. Tip the mixture into the tin and spread into the corners in an even layer.

4 Bake for 15–20 minutes until just beginning to colour around the edges. (The mixture will still be very soft but will harden as it cools.) Leave to cool in the tin.

5 Lift the flapjack out of the tin in one piece and cut into fingers.

Cook's Tip
Don't be tempted to overcook flapjacks; they'll turn crisp and dry and lose their lovely chewy texture.

No-bake Heaven

When you say cookies, most people think of baking – but this chapter proves that you don't need to go near an oven to make fabulous cookies. It is packed with wonderful ideas that kids will love, from peanut-butter flavoured wafer wedges and mini crispy cookies to white chocolate snowballs and cute little pink piglets.

Chocolate Crispy Cookies

These little chocolate-coated cornflake cakes are always a hit with kids. They couldn't be easier to make – and are great for young aspiring cooks who want to get involved in the kitchen. The only problem is giving the mixture time to set before they've been gobbled up by hungry helpers.

4 Remove the bowl from the heat and tip in the cornflakes. Mix well until the cornflakes are thoroughly coated in the chocolate mixture.

5 Place a 6.5cm/2½in round cutter on the paper and put a spoonful of the chocolate mixture in the centre. Pack down firmly with the back of the spoon to make a thick cookie.

6 Gently ease away the cutter, using the spoon to help keep the mixure in place. Continue making cookies in this way until all the mixture has been used up. Chill for 1 hour.

7 Spread out a little icing sugar on a plate. Lift each cookie from the paper and lightly roll the edges in the icing sugar to finish.

Makes 16

90g/3½oz milk chocolate
15ml/1 tbsp golden (light corn) syrup
90g/3½oz/2 cups cornflakes
icing (confectioners') sugar, for dusting

1 Line a large tray or baking sheet with baking parchment.

2 Break the chocolate into a large heatproof bowl and add the syrup. Rest the bowl over a pan of gently simmering water and leave until melted, stirring frequently.

3 Put the cornflakes in a plastic bag and, using a rolling pin, lightly crush the cornflakes, breaking them into fairly small pieces.

Chocolate Nut Slice

Children will love this combination of chunky broken cookies, chocolate and nuts. Although the unsliced bar looks small, it is very rich so is best sliced very thinly. You could use any other plain cookies in this recipe, or substitute hazelnuts or brazil nuts for the almonds, if you like.

Makes 10 slices

225g/8oz milk chocolate
40g/1½oz/3 tbsp unsalted (sweet) butter, diced
75g/3oz rich tea biscuits (plain cookies)
50g/2oz/½ cup flaked (sliced) almonds
75g/3oz plain (semisweet) or white chocolate, roughly chopped
icing (confectioners') sugar, for dusting

1 Break the milk chocolate into pieces and place in a heatproof bowl with the butter. Rest the bowl over a pan of simmering water and stir frequently until melted.

2 Meanwhile, dampen a 450g/1lb loaf tin (pan) and line the base and sides with clear film (plastic wrap). Don't worry about smoothing out the creases in the film.

3 When the chocolate has melted, remove it from the heat and leave for 5 minutes until slightly cooled.

4 Break the biscuits into small pieces, then stir into the melted chocolate with the almonds. Add the chopped chocolate into the bowl and fold in quickly and lightly.

5 Turn the mixture into the tin and pack down with a fork. Tap the base of the tin gently on the work surface. Chill for 2 hours until set.

6 To serve, turn the chocolate loaf on to a board and peel away the clear film. Dust lightly with icing sugar and slice thinly.

Chocolate Birds' Nests

These delightful crispy chocolate nests make a perfect Easter teatime treat and are a real favourite with kids. They're so quick and easy to make and young children can have great fun shaping the chocolate mixture inside the paper cases and tucking the pastel-coloured eggs inside.

Makes 12

200g/7oz milk chocolate
25g/1oz/2 tbsp unsalted (sweet)
  butter, diced
90g/3½oz shredded wheat cereal
36 small pastel-coloured, sugar-coated
  chocolate eggs

Cook's Tip

Bags of sugar-coated chocolate eggs are widely available in supermarkets at Easter time. However, if you have trouble finding them out of season, try an old-fashioned sweet (candy) store. They often have large jars of this type of sweet, which they sell all year round.

I Line the sections of a tartlet tin (muffin pan) with 12 decorative paper cake cases.

2 Break the milk chocolate into pieces and put in a bowl with the butter. Rest the bowl over a pan of gently simmering water and stir frequently until melted. Remove the bowl from the heat and leave to cool for a few minutes.

3 Using your fingers, crumble the Shredded Wheat into the melted chocolate. Stir well until the cereal is completely coated in chocolate.

4 Divide the mixture among the paper cases, pressing it down gently with the back of a spoon. Make a slight indentation in the centre. Tuck three eggs into each nest and leave to set for about 2 hours.

White Chocolate Snowballs

These little spherical cookies are particularly popular during the festive season. They're simple to make, yet utterly delicious and bursting with creamy, buttery flavours. If you like, make them in advance of a special tea as they will keep well in the refrigerator for a few days.

Makes 16

200g/7oz white chocolate
25g/1oz/2 tbsp butter, diced
90g/3½oz/generous 1 cup desiccated
    (dry unsweetened shredded) coconut
90g/3½oz syrup sponge or
    Madeira cake
icing (confectioners') sugar, for dusting

1 Break the chocolate into pieces and put in a heatproof bowl with the butter. Rest the bowl over a pan of gently simmering water and stir frequently until melted. Remove the bowl from the heat and set aside for a few minutes.

2 Meanwhile, put 50g/2oz/⅔ cup of the coconut on a plate and set aside. Crumble the sponge or cake and add to the melted chocolate with the remaining coconut. Mix well to form a chunky paste.

3 Take spoonfuls of the mixture and roll into balls, about 2.5cm/1in in diameter, and immediately roll them in the reserved coconut. Place the balls on greaseproof (waxed) paper and leave to set.

4 To serve, dust the snowballs with plenty of icing sugar.

Cook's Tip
You'll need to shape the mixture into balls as soon as you've mixed in the coconut and sponge or cake; the mixture sets very quickly and you won't be able to shape it once it hardens.

Pink Piggies

These are what you could call rainy day cookies. They are fun to make and thoroughly absorbing when the family is stuck indoors. You might want to make up icings in other colours and experiment with your own animal variations. Children's books are a great source of inspiration.

Makes 10

90g/3½oz/scant 1 cup icing (confectioners') sugar, plus extra for dusting
50g/2oz/¼ cup unsalted (sweet) butter, at room temperature, diced
10 rich tea (plain cookies) or digestive biscuits (graham crackers)
200g/7oz white ready-to-roll icing
pink food colouring
small, pink soft sweets (candies)
tube of black writer icing

1 To make the buttercream, put the icing sugar and butter in a bowl and beat with a hand-held electric whisk until smooth, pale and creamy.

2 Using a small palette knife (metal spatula) spread the rich tea or digestive biscuits almost to the edges with the buttercream.

3 Reserve 25g/1oz of the ready-to-roll icing and add a few drops of the pink food colouring to the remainder. Knead on a clean work surface that has been lightly dusted with icing sugar until the pink colouring is evenly distributed.

4 Reserve about 25g/1oz of the pink icing. If necessary, lightly dust your work surface with more icing sugar and roll out the remaining pink icing very thinly.

5 Using a cookie cutter that is just slightly smaller than the rich tea or digestive biscuits, cut out rounds of pink icing. Lay a round over each cookie and press it down gently on to the buttercream.

6 Halve 5 of the pink sweets and press into an oval shape. Make two small holes in each one with a wooden skewer or cocktail stick (toothpick) to make a nose.

7 Using a little of the buttercream, attach a halved sweet to the centre of each cookie.

8 Using the black writer icing, pipe two small dots of icing above the nose to resemble eyes, then pipe a small, curved mouth.

9 Thinly roll out the reserved pink icing and the reserved white icing. Dampen the white icing with a little water and press the pink icing gently on top. Using a small sharp knife, cut out triangles for ears.

10 Dampen one edge of the ears with a little water and secure, pink side up, to the cookies. Gently curl the ears out at the ends.

Cook's Tip
If you cannot get black writer icing, use any dark food colouring such as black, blue or brown and paint on the features with a fine brush.

Apricot and Coconut Kisses

These tangy, fruity treats make a colourful addition to the tea table. Although they are easy to make and can be mixed and shaped in a matter of a few minutes, remember to allow plenty of time for the apricots to soak, and also for the kisses to chill before serving.

Makes 12

130g/4½oz/generous ½ cup ready-to-eat
  dried apricots
100ml/3½fl oz/scant ½ cup orange juice
40g/1½oz/3 tbsp unsalted (sweet)
  butter, at room temperature, diced
75g/3oz/¾ cup icing (confectioners')
  sugar, plus extra for dusting (optional)
90g/3½oz/generous 1 cup desiccated
  (dry unsweetened shredded) coconut,
  lightly toasted
2 glacé (candied) cherries, cut
  into wedges

1 Finely chop the dried apricots, then tip them into a bowl. Pour in the orange juice and leave to soak for about 1 hour until all the juice has been absorbed.

2 In a large bowl, beat together the butter and sugar with a wooden spoon until pale and creamy.

3 Gradually add the soaked apricots to the creamed butter and sugar mixture, beating well after each addition, then stir in the toasted coconut.

4 Line a small baking tray with greaseproof (waxed) paper.

5 Place teaspoonfuls of the coconut mixture on to the paper, piling them up into little pyramid shapes. Gently press the mixture together with your fingers to form neat shapes.

6 Top each kiss with a tiny wedge of cherry, gently pressing it into the mixture. Chill the kisses for about 1 hour until firm, then serve lightly dusted with a little icing sugar, if you like.

Cook's Tip

It is essential that all the orange juice has been absorbed by the apricots before adding them to the butter mixture, otherwise the kisses will be too moist to set properly.

Sweet Peanut Wafers

Delicate wafers filled with a sweet, peanut-flavoured buttercream make a fun, no-bake recipe that kids of any age can help with. Just remember to chill the wafer sandwiches after they have been assembled, otherwise they will be almost impossible to cut.

Makes 12

65g/2½oz/4 tbsp unsalted (sweet) butter, at room temperature, diced
65g/2½oz/generous ½ cup icing (confectioners') sugar
115g/4oz/½ cup crunchy peanut butter
12 fan-shaped wafers
50g/2oz plain (semisweet) chocolate

1 Put the butter and sugar in a bowl and beat with a hand-held electric whisk until very light and creamy. Beat in the peanut butter.

2 Using a small palette knife (metal spatula), spread a thick layer of the mixture on to a wafer and spread to the edges.

3 Place another wafer on top of the peanut buttercream and press it down very gently. Spread the top wafer with more buttercream, then place another wafer on top and press down gently.

4 Use the remaining buttercream and wafers to assemble three more fans in the same way. Spread any remaining buttercream around the sides of the fans. Chill for at least 30 minutes until firm.

5 Using a serrated knife, carefully slice each fan into three equal wedges and arrange in a single layer on a small tray.

6 Break the chocolate into pieces and put in a heatproof bowl placed over a pan of gently simmering water. Stir frequently until melted.

7 Remove the bowl from the heat and leave to stand for a few minutes to cool slightly.

8 Drizzle lines of chocolate over the wafers, then leave to set in a cool place for at least 1 hour.

Cookies for Special Diets

Some children need to avoid foods that contain either gluten or dairy products due to allergy or intolerance. This chapter is dedicated to terrific, tasty cookies that avoid problem ingredients. So, even if your child is following a special diet, they won't have to miss out on the fun.

Rocky Road Wedges

Free from gluten and wheat, these crumbly chocolate wedges contain home-made popcorn in place of broken cookies, which are the classic ingredient in no-bake cookies such as this. To make a version that is dairy free, too, use a non-dairy margarine in place of the butter.

Makes 8

15ml/1 tbsp vegetable oil
25g/1oz/2½ tbsp popping corn
150g/5oz orange-flavoured plain (semisweet) chocolate
25g/1oz/2 tbsp unsalted (sweet) butter, diced
75g/3oz soft vanilla fudge, diced
icing (confectioners') sugar, for dusting

Cook's Tip
When buying products such as chocolate or fudge, always check the label to make sure they are gluten-free.

1 Heat the oil in a heavy pan. Add the popping corn, cover with a lid and heat, shaking the pan once or twice, until the popping noises die down. (It is important not to lift the lid until the popping stops.)

2 Remove the pan from the heat and leave for about 30 seconds before removing the lid. Be careful, as there may be quite a lot of steam trapped inside. Transfer the popcorn to a bowl and leave to cool for about 5 minutes.

3 Meanwhile, line the base of an 18cm/7in sandwich tin (pan).

4 Once cooled, tip the corn into a plastic bag and tap with a rolling pin to break up into small pieces.

5 Break the chocolate into a heatproof bowl. Add the butter and rest the bowl over a pan of gently simmering water. Stir frequently until melted. Remove the bowl from the heat and leave to cool for 2 minutes.

6 Stir the popcorn and fudge into the chocolate until well coated, then turn the mixture into the tin and press down firmly in an even layer. Leave to set for about 30 minutes.

7 Turn the cookie out on to a board and cut into eight wedges. Serve lightly dusted with sugar.

Meringue Squiggles

Free from gluten, wheat and cow's milk, these wiggly wands are great for children's parties. They are fun to shape and eat, and kids of all ages love making and decorating them. Be sure to check that the multi-coloured sprinkles are free from gluten and cow's milk.

Makes 14–16

2 egg whites
90g/3½oz/½ cup caster
(superfine) sugar
45ml/3 tbsp icing (confectioners') sugar
multi-coloured sugar sprinkles,
to decorate

1 Preheat the oven to 150°C/300°F/ Gas 2. Line a large baking sheet with baking parchment.

2 Put the egg whites in a large, clean bowl and whisk with a hand-held electric whisk until they form firm peaks.

3 Add a spoonful of caster sugar to the whisked egg whites and whisk for about 15 seconds to combine. Add another spoonful and whisk again. Continue in this way until all the sugar has been added.

4 Spoon the meringue mixture into a large piping (pastry) bag fitted with a large plain nozzle. Alternatively, spoon the mixture into a plastic bag, gently push it into one corner and snip off the tip so that the meringue can be pushed out in a 2cm/¾in-thick line.

5 Pipe neat, wavy lines of meringue, about 13cm/5in long, on to the baking sheet, then bake for about 1 hour until dry and crisp.

6 Carefully peel the meringues off the baking parchment and transfer to a wire rack to cool.

7 Put the icing sugar in a small bowl and mix in a few drops of water to make a smooth paste.

8 Using a fine pastry brush, brush the tops of the meringues with a little of the sugar paste, then scatter over the multi-coloured sugar sprinkles to decorate.

Big Macs

These giant macaroons are crisp on the outside, chewy in the middle and naturally free from gluten and cow's milk. Ground almonds can be a great alternative to the wheat flour used in most cookies, and macaroons don't need butter for their deliciously moist, rich taste.

Makes 9

2 egg whites
5ml/1 tsp almond essence (extract)
115g/4oz/1 cup ground almonds
130g/4½oz/generous 1 cup light
    muscovado (brown) sugar

Cook's Tips

• *These macaroons will store well in an airtight container; do not store in the refrigerator because they'll turn soft and lose their lovely crisp and chewy texture.*
• *To make a macaroon with a milder flavour, use caster (superfine) sugar in place of the light muscovado sugar.*

1 Preheat the oven to 180°C/350°F/ Gas 4. Line a large baking sheet with baking parchment. Put the egg whites in a large, clean bowl and whisk until they form stiff peaks.

2 Add the almond essence to the egg whites and whisk to combine. Sprinkle over the ground almonds and sugar and gently fold in using a large metal spoon.

3 Place nine spoonfuls of the mixture, spacing them well apart, on to the baking sheet and flatten slightly. Bake for 15 minutes until risen, deep golden and beginning to turn crisp.

4 Leave the macaroons on the baking sheet for 5 minutes, then transfer to a wire rack to cool.

Shortbread Ring Cookies

Decorated with colourful chopped sweets, these little gluten- and dairy-free cookies are great for younger kids. They make delicious lunch box fillers or snacks during the day. Don't forget to check the ingredients on the jellied fruit sweets as some varieties could contain gluten.

Makes 8–10

150g/5oz/1¼ cups gluten-free flour
90g/3½oz/½ cup rice flour
finely grated rind of 1 lemon
75g/3oz/6 tbsp dairy-free margarine
50g/2oz/¼ cup caster (superfine) sugar
1 egg yolk
10ml/2 tsp water

FOR THE TOPPING

90g/3½oz/scant 1 cup icing
    (confectioners') sugar
50g/2oz/½ cup dairy-free margarine
small jellied fruit sweets (candies)

1 Put the gluten-free flour, rice flour, lemon rind and margarine in a food processor and process briefly to combine. Add the sugar, egg yolk and water and mix to a dough.

2 Turn the dough on to a lightly floured surface and knead. Wrap in clear film (plastic wrap) and chill for about 30 minutes.

3 Preheat the oven to 180°C/350°F/ Gas 4. Grease a baking sheet.

4 Roll out the dough on a lightly floured surface to a thickness of about 5mm/¼in.

5 Using a 6.5cm/2½in plain or fluted cutter, cut out rounds and place on the baking sheet. Using a 4cm/1½in round cutter, cut out and remove the centre of each round.

6 Bake for about 20 minutes until beginning to turn pale golden. Leave on the baking sheet for 2 minutes then transfer to a wire rack to cool.

7 To make the topping, put the icing sugar and margarine in a bowl and beat together until creamy.

8 Pipe or spoon the topping on to the ring cookies. Chop the jellied sweets into small pieces with a pair of scissors and gently press them into the cream to decorate.

Almond Jumbles

This gluten-free mixture of oats and ground almonds makes a typically chunky, crumbly cookie, packed with plenty of flavour and texture. To make a dairy-free version, use a non-dairy margarine in place of the butter. The sweet, sticky jam filling is always a favourite with kids, making these cookies a much appreciated afternoon treat.

Makes 20

130g/4½oz/9 tbsp unsalted (sweet)
 butter, at room temperature, diced
130g/4½oz/generous ½ cup light
 muscovado (brown) sugar
1 egg, lightly beaten
5ml/1 tsp almond essence (extract)
130g/4½oz/generous 1 cup
 gluten-free flour
5ml/1 tsp bicarbonate of soda
 (baking soda)
130g/4½oz/1¼ cups rolled oats
50g/2oz/½ cup ground almonds
75–90ml/5–6 tbsp strawberry jam
icing (confectioners') sugar, for dusting

1 Preheat the oven to 190°C/375°F/ Gas 5. Grease two baking sheets.

2 Put the butter and sugar into a large bowl and beat with a hand-held whisk until pale and creamy.

3 Add the egg and almond essence to the butter and sugar mixture and beat until well combined.

4 Sift the flour and bicarbonate of soda into a separate bowl, then add the rolled oats and ground almonds and stir to combine.

5 Tip the oat mixture into the creamed butter and sugar mixture and stir until thoroughly combined.

6 Place spoonfuls of the mixture on to the baking sheets, spaced slightly apart to allow room for spreading. Dip a thumb in gluten-free flour and use to make a shallow indentation in the top of each cookie.

7 Bake for about 15 minutes until the cookies are risen and golden.

8 Leave the cookies on the baking sheets for about 3 minutes to firm up slightly, then transfer to wire racks to cool completely.

9 To serve, spoon a little jam into the indentation on the top of each cookie, then dust with icing sugar.

Cherry Coconut Squares

These colourful gluten- and dairy-free cookies are quick and easy to prepare and make an excellent standby for unexpected guests. Try to use cherry jam for the filling but, if you don't have any in the kitchen, you can use any other type of red jam – the chunkier the better. If you have a loose-based baking tin, it will make turning these out much easier to do.

Makes 9

130g/4½oz/generous 1 cup
  gluten-free flour
90g/3½oz/½ cup non-dairy margarine
50g/2oz/⅔ cup desiccated (dry
  unsweetened shredded) coconut, plus
  an extra 30ml/2 tbsp toasted,
  for sprinkling
50g/2oz/¼ cup caster
  (superfine) sugar
5ml/1 tsp vanilla essence (extract)
90ml/6 tbsp cherry jam
90g/3½oz/scant ½ cup glacé (candied)
  cherries, chopped
icing (confectioners') sugar,
  for dusting

1 Preheat the oven to 160°C/325°F/ Gas 3. Grease an 18cm/7in square shallow baking tin (pan), and line the base with greaseproof (waxed) paper or baking parchment.

2 Place the flour and margarine in a food processor and process for a minute or two until the mixture just starts to bind together.

3 Add the coconut, caster sugar and vanilla essence and blend until thoroughly combined.

4 Tip the mixture into the tin and spread into the corners, pressing down and flattening with a fork. Bake for 25–30 minutes until pale golden. Leave to cool in the tin.

5 Spread the cookie base with the jam, then carefully lift out of the tin.

6 Place the jam-covered cookie base on a board and, using a large, sharp knife, carefully cut into nine even-sized squares.

7 Scatter chopped cherries over each square and sprinkle with the toasted coconut. Serve lightly dusted with icing sugar.

Cook's Tip

Some brands of glacé cherries may contain gluten, so always check the label. If you prefer, you can use any other type of dried fruit instead. For example, use apricot jam and chopped dried apricots in place of the cherry jam and glacé cherries.

index